"AND THIS IS SAN DIEGO...

It is a city of magic, mystic with charm of salt water and sloping shores, of pure air from neighboring mountains mingling with the perfumed breath of the desert, riotous with health! Every sort of flower blooms amazingly, lending more beauty and fragrance to the mellow atmosphere; and every sort of fruit grows more luscious under the benign influence of daily sun-filled skies and splendid starry nights.

Army and navy men on land and sea, or in the air, add a touch of martial gaiety to a city already blessed with native loveliness, where leisure and industry walk hand in hand with progress and romance. And the Bay is proud to wait the coming of the Fleet, as the toiling waters of the great blue Pacific urge it home.

For peace and rest from busy world activities, for blithe and merry times of free warm zest in life, the very tones of the great pipe organ in beautiful Balboa Park peal forth an urgent invitation, and those who once accept it hold henceforth a not-to-be-forgotten joy of heart."

Peter A. Lea, 1932

A COMSTOCK EDITION

SAN DIEGO AND THE BACK COUNTRY

Edited by

Davis Dutton

A Westways / Comstock Edition

1972

BALLANTINE BOOKS • NEW YORK
An Intext Publisher

BALLANTINE BOOKS, INC.
101 Fifth Avenue, New York, N.Y. 10003

And this is San Diego—gold and blue and green, like a joyous and convivial holiday.

What your heart yearned for, what you have always hoped to find—here in San Diego it envelops you. Maybe it's the far blue arc of the horizon where water meets sky. Maybe it's the great quiet harbor where hundreds of craft ride at safe anchor. Maybe it's the drive along the Strand. Maybe it's the lights gleaming from Point Loma. Maybe it's colorful Coronado, unchanged for a generation. Maybe it's the Torrey pines. Maybe it's old Mexico beckoning a welcome. Maybe it's the people; cultured, gentle, unhurried. Maybe it is all of these, and much more—but it is here, the deep, glad feeling of home.

It is a city of magic—mystic with charm of salt water and sloping shores, of pure air from neighboring mountains mingling with the perfumed breath of the desert—riotous with health! Every sort of flower blooms amazingly, lending more beauty and fragrance to the mellow atmosphere; and every sort of fruit grows more luscious under the benign influence of daily sun-filled skies and splendid starry nights.

Army and navy men, active on land and sea, or in the air, add a touch of martial gayety to a city already blessed with native loveliness, where leisure and industry walk hand in hand with progress and romance. And the Bay is proud to wait the coming of the Fleet, as the toiling waters of the great blue Pacific urge it home.

For peace and rest from busy world activities, for blithe and merry times of free warm zest in life, the very tones of the great pipe organ in beautiful Balboa Park peal forth an urgent invitation—and those who once accept it hold henceforth a not-to-be-forgotten joy of heart.

PETER A. LEA, 1932

Contents

Note

The selections in *San Diego and the Back Country* have been gleaned from *Westways* magazine over the sixty year period from 1909 to 1969.

They have been chosen to portray the life and times of San Diego County from its origins to the present time; its remarkable variety of landscape, its unique place in California's development, its people, and the historical events which have formed it.

This collection should satisfy both the random browser through its pages and the one who reads it from cover to cover. Old restaurant reviews, famous San Diego "firsts," stories of the World Fairs in San Diego, and early accounts of "motor car adventures" are included, along with articles from some of the best writing talents of the West—Jerry MacMullen, Philip Johnston, Judy Van der Veer, Farnsworth Crowder, Russ Leadabrand, Carey McWilliams (who later went East to edit *The Nation*), John Walton Caughey, and Lawrence Clark Powell. The total effect will be to give the reader a portrait of San Diego that will not be found elsewhere.

San Diego and the Back Country

I

In the Beginning

—————◆◆◆————

San Diego County occupies a special place in America—geographically and historically. Tucked neatly at the extreme southwest portion of the U.S., it borders the Pacific Ocean on the west and the Republic of Mexico on the south. It has a large natural harbor, recognized by the navigator Cabrillo, who put into port there in 1542. Father Junípero Serra in 1769 thought it a fine place to build the first California mission. And long before that, migrating Stone Age peoples were sufficiently impressed by the climate, topography and natural gifts of San Diego to cease migrating and settle down there—something Atomic Age peoples continue to do. The articles and excerpts that follow give glimpses of the events which have made that region down in the lower left-hand corner of the map unique.

"A Landlocked and Very Good Harbor"

Jerry MacMullen

It was a mere 50 years after the historic voyage of Columbus when João Rodrigues Cabrilho, a Portuguese navigator sailing for Spain, set out from the little port of Navidad on the west coast of Mexico to explore the unknown shores to the north and, hopefully, to reach the Orient. The date was June 27, 1542.

It took him more than three months to reach San Diego, which is not surprising when you consider his tiny ships, the *San Salvador* and the *Victoria*. Locally built by soldiers and amateurs, they were a bit on the crude side, and they call to mind that old chantey about the ". . . soldiers and tinkers and tailors and all, who shipped as prime sailors, aboard the Black Ball."

Cabrilho—or Cabrillo, as he is more widely known —made landfall on September 28 and named it San Miguel. He called it "a landlocked and very good harbor" and sent a detail ashore in search of fresh water. . . .

Cabrillo pushed on to the north with his pathetic little ships, got far up the coast and returned to winter quarters in the Channel Islands. By the opening days of 1543, he was dead of injuries received while landing through the surf, and his grave has never been found. But he made history; he was the first European to set foot on the coast of Alta California. And in his wake would follow at long last the Yankee hide ships, Pacific Mail's wooden steamers, big steel-hulled windjammers via Cape Horn and up from the antipodes, and cargo and passenger ships of every sort. . . .

Cabrillo's ships and men returned home, and nothing was done about their discoveries for sixty years. Then came Sebastián Vizcaíno, on November 10, 1602; he had been sent out to check on the reports of Cabrillo's expedition and was ordered not to change any of the names on their crude maps. But, on the claim that his predecessor's navigation and records were so vague that he could recognize few places from them, he engaged in name changing on a wholesale basis—including calling Cabrillo's first landing spot San Diego instead of San Miguel.

He came back to New Spain with glowing reports; it would be a grand place for Spanish expansion. The top brass agreed to think it over. They were still thinking it over some one hundred sixty-six years later when disquieting rumors began to trickle in that Russia might make passes at Alta California, which would be bad— or that England might, which would be worse. So, in 1768, it was decided to outfit an expedition by land and by sea to meet at San Diego. Don Gaspar de Portolá was placed in overall command.

Early in 1769, three ships got away from La Paz, down near the tip of Baja California; they were the *San Carlos,* the *San Antonio* and the *San José.* And to the last named—and smallest—of the trio goes the grim distinction of being the first vessel in the San Diego trade to leave port and simply vanish with all hands; she was never seen again.

The *San Antonio* arrived first, although she had sailed a month or more after the *San Carlos.* She got in on April 11. Two of her crew had died en route, and many others were in a bad way from scurvy. The *San Carlos* showed up on April 29 with only four of her crew still on their feet, but somehow they managed to get all hands ashore to a crude camp near what now is Pacific Highway.

Meanwhile, the land elements of the expedition—and they were having no circus, either—were approaching from the south. On May 14 the advance party, under Captain Fernando de Rivera y Moncada, arrived, and the camp was at once moved to higher and healthier land, out near what now is called Presidio Hill. Portolá arrived June 29, followed closely by the dedicated Franciscan who would found the long chain of missions of Alta California, Father Junípero Serra.

The work of building the permanent presidio went on, and on July 16, 1769, Father Serra established the first of the missions, San Diego de Alcalá. It was one of the presidio buildings, and events were soon to prove that it was too far from tillable farmland—and too close to the soldiers. Not waiting for the dedication of the mission, Portolá pushed on to the north, looking for Monterey. He missed it the first time—or rather, he found it but could not reconcile the terrain with Vizcaíno's florid description—and he returned to San Diego. After that, he became pretty well fed up with the whole operation. Supplies were dangerously low when the *San Antonio* popped in on her way to Monterey where, her people supposed, Portolá was in business. So Portolá went back, this time successfully, and his opinion of the records left by the man who had so severely criticized poor old Cabrillo may well be imagined.

The fine new mission, on its present site a few miles up the river valley, was established early in October of 1775, but a month later was sacked and burned by a howling mob of some 800 Indians, who murdered Fr. Luís Jayme and several others. While all this was going on, the presidio garrison peacefully slumbered. Two years passed before the mission was rebuilt. . . .

The first American ship to call was the *Betsy* on

August 25, 1800, and she appears to have behaved herself, as did the *Enterprise* the next summer. Thus, lulled into a false sense of security, the Spanish believed the master of the *Alexander* when he told a pitiful tale of scurvy and other hardships, on February 26, 1803, and asked if he might come in and rest up a bit. Later they caught him red-handed trying to smuggle out sea otter pelts, so they gave him the bum's rush. A fortnight later, the *Lelia Byrd*'s people asked permission to replenish their supply of water and firewood—and immediately got involved in smuggling out sea otter pelts. There followed a bit of activism that included the roughing up of some Spanish soldiers and the exchange of cannonry between Fort Guijarros and the hastily departing *Lelia Byrd*. Only once more did San Diego's harbor defenses fire in anger; in 1828, the fort—then controlled by the Mexicans—opened up on the *Franklin*, which had been ordered held while the legality of her general behavior in California waters might be examined. The skipper of the *Franklin*, resenting the search order, ran for it and escaped.

The transfer of San Diego from Spanish to Mexican rule in 1822 was little more than a formality; one flag down, another flag up. The ships continued to call, bringing in Yankee and European goods and taking out pelts, hides and tallow. Of the 31 vessels arriving between 1800 and 1828, 16 were American, six Russian, four British, three Hawaiian, one Spanish and one French. And to handle more effectively the growing trade in hides and tallow, the first of the hide houses was built at La Playa in 1829 to take care of the cargo of hides being assembled for the ship *Brookline*. It was here that the first American flag in San Diego, if not indeed in all of California, was raised. It was crudely made from bits of clothing of whatever appropriate color; the Mexican authorities were not amused.

Too far from that period's Mexican version of the Pentagon to get much attention, the presidio began to go downhill in more ways than one. With Indian attacks no longer the threat that they once were, soldiers began to plant modest little gardens at the foot of the hill, and modest houses also began to appear. On December 21, 1834, an election was held—there were 13 votes cast—and San Diego chose its first *ayuntamiento* or town council. They took office January 1, 1835, and San Diego, which so far had been merely a military post, became a city.

(1969)

Diego and the Hermit
Michael R. O'Neil

Seville is a city of some magic. The word alone pricks the most lethargic mind to dreams. There are the graceful and crisp-voiced señoritas and the sun-carpeted patios with their tinkling fountains and flowers, and the mosque . . . with its glistening dome and tall . . . minarets that pointed starward in the twelfth century, when the Mohammedans would hear the muezzin's call to prayer.

It is old, that city; and, as if a genii's finger had tapped at the font of romance, to merely mention Seville is to draw white rabbits out of a top-hat like a magician. As a white rabbit so emerging from romance-packed Seville, San Diego de Alcalá stands framed eternally in his long skirted Franciscan frock. True, if he was not born at Seville, he was born so near it that a walk would take him there. The little town of San Nicolás del Puerto lay fifteen leagues away. There San Diego first opened his eyes upon a world that was to treat him to immortality.

America had not been discovered when San Diego was born. It would be something over a half century before it was discovered—before, that is to say, Columbus sailed the seas in his small ship like a thimble on the ocean—and some 277 years later the mission of San Diego in California was to be jotted down as founded in history. . . .

But to turn back the clock: San Diego was born of the poorer classes in Spain toward the end of the fourteenth century. It was during the period when Spanish literature was Moorish.

Moorish influence pressed strongly everywhere; dominantly pushed itself forward.

* * *

No wealth lay in the family of Diego. . . . They were honest, ignorant, and faithful country folk, resigned to their lot upon earth, and hopeful of heaven one day. No more.

San Diego in his early youth, this awkward peasant boy, strayed off to make the company of a hermit priest . . . a man who, when not occupied with God, was occupied with his spade, turning over the earth that his lettuce might the better thrive and his melons take color in his garden. Or the two would sit in the morning sunlight to make use of their hands in shaping wooden spoons or bowls, and such like. In this way they earned sufficient to keep themselves alive.

* * *

The life of the hermit pleased San Diego for a little while, for several years in fact, then he went away to enter the convent of the Franciscans at Arrizafa. He was given a position among the lay brothers as a menial. . . . He peeled vegetables and stirred stew. Murillo, in one of his famous paintings of Diego for the Franciscans, pictures him kneeling in the act of blessing a copper pot of broth. Simplicity was this man's password into sainthood.

. . .

Now, it is a far cry from Seville to the Canary Islands. But in the Canary Islands we are to see San Diego next.

. . .

Bold and picturesque these islands loom from the sea. In clear weather the snow-capped peak that dominates the island of Teneriffe . . . is visible for many miles around. It is volcanic, only now partially extinct. The natives considered it the residence of the evil one.

. . .

In the Canary Islands San Diego was apt at teaching, so it is said, the rudiments of Christianity to the natives. One can readily believe this. He, himself, was close to them in his childlike simplicity and would doubtless have been more successful than some more brilliant scholar put to the same task. At Fuerteventura, one of the islands of this group, San Diego was appointed superior of the Franciscan convent. It sounds perhaps more inspiring than it was. The island was a new foundling in the arms of Spain. There was not much to be seen of civilization. Later he returned to Spain.

But he was to travel again. In 1450 we see him journeying to Rome. Returning to Spain again he spent something over the next ten years of his life in the Franciscan establishments of Castile and Seville. . . .

It was at Alcala where he died in 1463. Around his bed gathered his brother friars . . . and with a crucifix in hand he implored them to pardon him "for any scandal he might have given them!"

As for the rest, one may quote the living Franciscan in California, Father Zephyrin Englehardt: "All were deeply touched, while tears welled from the eyes of the dying saint. Then fixing his eyes on the crucifix, he repeated with great tenderness the words of the hymn of the Cross, '*Dulce lignum, dulces clavos,*' and quietly passed to his eternal reward."

Spain meanwhile rose to her height of glory, mistress of the world, with America as part of her royal domains. San Diego had not yet been canonized a saint. That was to come with the pleadings of Philip II. . . . During Philip's reign (1556-1621), his own son . . . Don Carlos (who, if truth were told, was not at all sane to begin with, and was forever in hot water) . . . was cured once of a "grievous wound" through the intercession of the long dead Diego, and King Philip in gratitude, it is said, determined to appeal to the Pope for Diego's formal canonization. And King Philip persisted until, in 1588, the bull was published, and Diego's title was now "Saint," or, in Spanish, *San* Diego.

(1932)

The Prehistoric Painter of Poway

H. H. Dunn

Whence he came, whither he went, what manner of man he was, or why he wandered, undoubtedly on foot and probably alone, through a particular, limited area of Southern California, no living man knows. But certain it is that, long before the days of the padres, a mysterious artist made and left an outdoor gallery of peculiar paintings in the hills of San Diego County.

From Escondido southward to the Mexican border—
beyond which his trail has not been followed—this
worker in oils left on the backbone of his world a series
of squares and rectangles ... occasionally accompanied
by rows of concentric crosses.

Painted in red, and always in red, these manuscripts
in stone are placed invariably on the flat, eastward-
facing surface of a granite boulder. ... In many, the
granite has eroded from beneath the paint, but the paint
remains, brittle, rather easily broken with the fingers,
yet apparently impervious to rain, wind and sun.

All of the paintings so far found are at or very near
the sites of the camps of the so-called "Scraper People"
—men still in the stone age, who are believed to have
preceded by a number of centuries the Indians who inhabited this section of California when white men arrived. ...

On other boulders, and on other granite faces, there
are the rather well known paintings of many-legged animals, birds, grasshoppers, men and curiously curved
lines, common to the "Indian paintings" of the Southwest. But apparently no other painter has dared to lay
his sacrilegious paints over what would seem to have
been paintings to the Sun God, on guard over the water
holes. No other painter has even dared to lay his colors
on the same boulders as that on which the "maze" remains. One ancient Mexican, who had lived in the
Poway Valley before the Indians were gathered to the
Pala and other reservations in San Diego and Riverside
counties, informed me that those Indians would not use
a camp site where the "square pattern," as he called it,
had been painted on a rock. He further told me that
there are at least a score of these paintings in the hills
along the Poway Valley, and that there are others across
the line in Lower California.

(1930)

1846: Battle at San Pasqual

John Walton Caughey

The battle of San Pasqual, an early morning encounter at a placid Indian village some forty miles northeast of San Diego, has the doubtful distinction of being California's bloodiest. This omits from consideration the Modoc War, which was a campaign rather than a battle. It also omits the Indian campaigns of the fifties, which were in reality massacres.

San Pasqual was a spur-of-the-moment, almost an accidental encounter. It did not decide the war with Mexico, or even the fate of California. It was not noteworthy for the generalship displayed, but it afforded unmistakable proof of the fighting ability of the Californians and it was an opportunity for great heroism by individual Americans.

On the day before the battle three military forces were converging in the quiet hill country near San Pasqual.

One was a band of eighty or one hundred native Californians led by Andrés Pico. They were partisans of the southern California revolt that had broken out at the pueblo of Los Angeles in September, and some of them had seen action in the battle of Chino and at Dominguez Rancho in the battle won by the Old Woman's Gun. They were splendid horsemen and well mounted. Not having enough firearms to go around, they had provided themselves with crude lances, knives lashed to poles. Their immediate mission was to harass a smaller American force that had sallied out from San Diego.

The Californians assumed that this force of about 40 men under Archibald Gillespie was on a foraging expedition. Actually, a courier had come into San Diego from Warner's Ranch to report the arrival there of the third force, a detachment of some one hundred ten United States dragoons under General Stephen Watts Kearny, nearing the end of its long march from Missouri and New Mexico. Gillespie's assignment was to conduct this force in, and, if feasible, to get them to strike at Pico's insurgents.

On Saturday, December 5, the two American forces established contact. Gillespie's men felt miserable enough. Most of the preceding night and all day they had slogged along through a cold rain. But the transcontinental travelers were much worse off. Their clothing was in tatters as well as being soaked through, many of them were without shoes, and they were so "perfectly exhausted" that at every halt some of them stretched out on the sodden ground. Their mules and horses were equally jaded.

In these circumstances the course of wisdom should have been to avoid battle, to hold the Californians off at a distance, with the field pieces if necessary, and to complete the march and join forces with Commodore Stockton's men at San Diego.

These Americans, however, were supremely confident and thoroughly disdainful of the Californians as fighting men. The attitude was plausible. After all, Kearny's dragoons were professional soldiers, the flower of the United States frontier forces. The Californians, besides being a pick-up group, were Mexicans, and doubtless quite like the ones who had failed to defend New Mexico. Kit Carson, who certainly knew his way around, said the Californians never had shown much fight, and Gillespie, in spite of his recent reverses at the hands of these same Californians, was full of swashbuckling confidence.

Consequently, although both men and mounts badly

needed a full night's rest, Kearny decided on an immediate attack. He assigned Major Swords and thirty dragoons to guard the baggage and another ten or fifteen men to stay with Gillespie's four-pounder. For the rest, boots and saddles sounded at 2 A.M. The night had cleared, but it was bitter cold, and the men, most of whom were still wet to the skin, shivered and grew numb.

After traveling about ten miles, they topped a rise and sighted the enemy's campfires. Kearny spoke a word of encouragement and ordered an attack by Captain Johnston and a dozen of the best mounted dragoons. They clattered down the hill and, with an Indian yell, spurred forward. The rest followed at the best speed they could get out of their mounts.

Had the Californians realized how large a force was arrayed against them, they doubtless would have fallen back before Johnston's charge. From the Indians they had heard of American troops arriving from the east, but the number of men riding in upon them was so small that they assumed they had only Gillespie's force to deal with. So they put up a stiff resistance. Johnston and some others were killed almost at once and the rest of his men were forced to turn back.

As they did so, the main body of Americans came into action, with Captain Moore leading a second charge. This time the Californians fell back and the Americans strung out in pursuit for half or three-quarters of a mile. It was all done with much spirit but with no precision. Then the California lancers rallied and rode back up the line and the real execution took place. With their guns wet or empty and useless except as clubs, the dragoons relied chiefly on their sabres. Massed in close formation they could have been effective, but they were badly scattered, everything was confused, the lancers were far better mounted, and particularly in retreat, the dragoons were easy targets.

Too late, the Americans rallied around one of the howitzers, and, when it was fired, the Californians withdrew. Day was just breaking. The Americans had possession of the battlefield, sometimes a token of victory, but their dead numbered eighteen, the wounded were as numerous, and hardly more than twice this many had gotten into the action. Surgeon John S. Griffin went to work cleaning and dressing the lance wounds, a task not completed until late afternoon. Others were detailed to collect the dead and dig a trench. After dark, Lieutenant Hammond having died of his wounds, these nineteen were buried in a common grave. Earlier in the day, messengers were dispatched to San Diego to appeal for help.

The next morning the march was resumed, with special guard and special care for the wounded. Pico's men hung about the column. Beyond Rancho San Bernardo they occupied a hill commanding the trail. In a spirited charge the Americans seized the hill and made camp. There was chicken broth for the invalids and stringy mule meat for the rest.

Because of the wounded they stayed in camp on the eighth. Chief event of the day was a flag of truce and an exchange of prisoners, whereby the Americans learned that their messengers had reached San Diego but that Stockton was not sending reinforcements. Kearny now wanted to march, no matter what the cost, but the naval officers persuaded him to wait until one more appeal could be made.

Kit Carson, Lieutenant Beale, and an Indian named Andrés were chosen to make the desperate effort. They managed to crawl through the picket line, but lost their boots in the process, and had to go barefoot, by dark, and by a roundabout route to San Diego. This time Stockton sent aid.

The stranded wayfarers, meanwhile, suffered tortures of thirst and hunger. On the tenth they buried Sergeant Cox. Later that day they foiled an attempt to stampede their stock and shot a fat mule which was a godsend after what they had been eating.

Finally, at about two o'clock on the morning of the eleventh the sentries at the hill camp heard the voices and the tramp of an approaching column. It turned out to be Lieutenant Gray with one hundred twenty sailors and eighty marines. They brought hardtack and jerky and formed a sufficient escort to conduct the survivors of San Pasqual into San Diego.

The toll of the battle, however, was not yet complete. On the nineteenth Joseph Kennedy succumbed to his wounds. Weeks later, Kearny, Gillespie, and some of the others were not yet recuperated, and in January Beale was not in condition to join the march toward Los Angeles.

Now a quiet valley given over to poultry farms, San Pasqual seems an improbable site for California's bitterest battle. The explanation, of course, is that nothing strategic determined that the battle should be at this spot. American troops happened to overtake a group of California insurgents here, and, with a tragic optimism which at the time appeared fully justified, General Kearny chose to precipitate the battle.

(1946)

Alonzo Horton's Dream

Harvey N. Wheat

"Alonzo, what in the world are you doing?" Mrs. Horton called as she rose sleepily on one elbow to get a better view of the figure bending over the table in the dining room.

"I'm choosing a site for my city, Sarah," her husband answered, as he bent closer to the atlas on the table.

A woman less accustomed to being disturbed in the middle of the night by a husband fired with dreams of building new cities might have been alarmed. But Mrs. Horton merely sighed and settled back in bed. After all, this wasn't the first time.

But she had hoped that when Alonzo had finished Hortonville, Wisconsin, he'd be satisfied to settle down with his furniture business in San Francisco. Founding cities might be all right for a man, but for a woman— well, Mrs. Horton preferred the security of San Francisco to the uncertainties of life in a new town.

But then, there was no use getting up at two o'clock in the morning to argue the matter. Maybe Alonzo would be more sensible with the return of daylight, she thought, as she drifted back to sleep.

For Alonzo there was no sleep, however. San Diego coursed through his mind like an electric current. San Diego could become one of the greatest cities on the Pacific Coast—that's what the speaker had said last night. It had the most healthful climate in the world, and the harbor was excellent. All it needed was a man with the courage and vision to develop it.

The next morning at breakfast when he presented his

plan to Mrs. Horton, she was outspoken in her disapproval. "Why can't you be satisfied with your furniture business?" she pleaded. To sell out a paying business and invest everything in a tract of sagebrush and cactus sounded like nonsense to her.

"You are too old, Alonzo," she argued. "At fifty-four you can't afford to risk your life's earnings that way."

But Alonzo's mind was made up. That night when he came home, he had already sold a large part of his stock.

A few days later, on April 15, 1867, Alonzo Erastus Horton sailed into San Diego Bay aboard the steamer *Pacific*—prepared to buy thirty or forty acres and start his city. When he walked into the sleepy little village of Old Town to inquire about land, he found that there was plenty of land—but no way of buying it.

It was public grazing land which no one could sell but the city trustees. And legally there were no city trustees. Being financially embarrassed, the pueblo had not held an election for several years.

With land to be bought and money in his pockets to but it, Alonzo Horton was not to be stopped by a thing like this.

"How much will it cost to call an election?" he inquired of the county clerk.

"Not less than $5.00," was the reply.

"Would you do it for ten?" Horton winked as he handed him $10 in gold.

Together he and the clerk wrote out the notices and tacked them up on nearby trees. The election was held, and the auctioneer opened bids on a 200-acre tract near the waterfront.

When Horton hesitantly called an opening bid of $100, the crowd was audibly amused. Thinking they were laughing because his bid was too low, Horton ventured to ask what the prevailing price of land was.

"Twenty dollars for good smooth land—$15 for rough," they told him.

From then on Horton did not bid so high, and when he figured up the total bill for the land for his city, the 1,000 acres had cost him $265.

Before laying out his city, he decided to return to San Francisco to get his wife and spread the glad news among his friends who might want to join in the venture. When he returned to San Diego, General Williams S. Rosecrans accompanied him.

Thrown into ecstasies by the possibilities of the site, Rosecrans returned to San Francisco, where his enthusiasm incited two capitalists to offer Horton $100,000 for his property, doubling the bid when he hesitated, and adding $50,000 more when he still appeared reluctant.

After due consideration Horton politely declined, however. If the land was worth that much, why not keep it and make the profits himself?

Within a few weeks survey stakes appeared among the cactus and sagebrush near the harbor, a wharf was built, and the listless residents of Old Town found themselves confronted with the opportunity of buying all the lots they wanted at $10 apiece.

Even at that price sales were slow. Old residents were wary; newcomers hesitated. Undaunted, Horton offered a large lot free to every man who would put up a house at least 12' by 16' by 12' and roof it with shingles or shakes. This offer brought results.

From then on it was one triumph after another. The price of lots doubled overnight, then tripled—and continued to rise.

Thousands of dollars a day was nothing; Horton received more than $1,000,000 from the sale of property.

In 1870 he built the famous Horton House, where he and his wife lived and where for the next several decades railroad magnates and capitalists met and made decisions of historic moment for San Diego. When the San Diego Bank was organized, Horton was elected president, but after a few months he resigned. He was doing more business than the bank was.

However, it was not a one-sided proposition with Horton. While he took in a fortune, he also gave away lots for churches, a courthouse and other public buildings, besides hundreds of lots to individuals for homes. . . . If Father Horton could sail into the harbor today, he would no doubt be mightily pleased with the progress his city has made since his death, and probably he would agree heartily with modern San Diegans who say, "When Horton started San Diego he really started something."

(1948)

The Band Plays in the Plaza

Jerry MacMullen

Across rutty D Street from the Horton House there was a wooden bandstand, where the City Guard Band appeared in the 1880's and 90's and poured out notes, not always sweet, from battered brass and woodwind. But be not hasty in your judgment of their music; did you ever try to keep a drooping mustache out of a piccolo?

The Horton House sprawled its dingily-painted front of brick, two stories high, all along D Street from Third to Fourth, and was the town's leading hostelry. To it came those travelers unable to make the financial grade to the Coronado, or who felt that the Brewster, a block away, and the Florence, up on the hill, were too far out in the country.

At times there were attractions other than the City Guard Band in the plaza fronting on the Horton House. From the hitching-rail on the far side to the very sidewalk of the hotel itself, the worthy citizens would gather to listen to the fiery patriotism of the Fourth of July orator, or to the solemn warnings of the dispenser of political dogma. On one occasion they had a county judge as the principal speaker. He was quite near-sighted, a bit absent-minded and an ardent devotee of eatin' tobacco. As the judge got up to speak, some scoundrel on the platform gently pushed the old gentleman's tophat, bottom up, from under his chair and out beside him. The judge warmed to his subject, felt the need of relief from tobacco juice. He looked down and saw the dark object on the floor at his side. And, dear myopic old chap that he was, he thought that it was a gaboon, and acted accordingly. The crowd loved it.

The punctured real-estate boom of the late 1880's brought headache and heartache. There were plenty of banks and other enterprises which folded up like so many tired concertinas. More than one business was sold to the insurance company on a dark night, while smoke and sparks mounted skyward. This was the era when the stock joke of the Los Angeles vaudevillians ran something like this:

"I just been down to San Diego, and the place is looking up."

"Looking up?" the stooge would reply, "Why—how's that?"

"Well sir, if you were flat on your back, I guess you'd be looking up too!"

It laid 'em in the aisles, every time.

But there was progress in the little town, even in those dark days when hardly a "steamer day" passed without witnessing truckloads of household goods plodding down to the wharf—and escape. Coal oil lamps gave way to gas, and the hissing Welsbach mantles in time moved on for electricity. In the outlying residence districts houses had their own gasplants—acetylene affairs which creaked and groaned dismally, but put out a very fair light from carbide and water.

In a corner of the gas house down by the bay, a long-legged Corliss engine drove the dynamo which fed a flickering current to the town's handful of carbon bulbs. They shut down every night at 12, to overhaul the engine—but of course, no honest, God-fearing citizen would stay up until after midnight, so what of it?

Horse cars and steam "dummies" were giving way now to cable cars, and right gorgeous cable cars they were. All atwinkle with nickel plate and stained glass, they might have just rolled out of the pages of Kipling's *Bow Flume Cable Car*. And they were named; yes, sir, named. No mere number was good enough for a San Diego cable car, so passengers rode up and down Fourth Street in the *Orizaba* and the *Montezuma*, and liked it.

Spluttering arc lights shed a lavenderish glow along the streets at night. In some parts of town these lights were carried in clusters at the tops of trussed steel masts some 120 feet high. Someone thought that the higher above the streets the better, so up they went. A man in a little wagon went around and lowered the lights each day to renew the carbons—except the tower lights, to which he had to climb in person. The burned-off ends of the carbons were collected by the youth of the city, who found them of just the right consistency for scribbling pictures and childish drolleries on the cement sidewalks.

Down in Chinatown, progress came slowly. Many of the buildings were equipped with auxiliary structures of the type made immortal by Mr. Chic Sale. Bad boys roamed the town in droves, when enforcement of the curfew law grew lax, and amused themselves by overturning these diminuitive edifices. It was more darned fun!

Along the north side of sandy B Street ran the B Street flume—a duct of many uses. Primarily a storm drain, it was merely a timbered ditch some five yards deep, covered with splintery planks at street level, and serving to carry the storm waters of Switzer Canyon down to the bay. But it had other, more noble uses. The firemen in the engine house at Tenth and B Streets used its plank surface as a drying rack for hose. And marauding brats, finding pursuit by whiskered, perspiring constabulary a bit too hot, found in it a haven, and an avenue of escape. All you had to do was slide through a scupper at the curb, drop down to the bottom of the flume, and go on about your business. At your own discretion and convenience, you could emerge a block or two up or down; or if the spirit moved you and the tide was out you could keep right on going until you came to the yellow sands of the bay, down by Regan's Bath House.

And there was the old B Street School, fronting on the flume. Its architecture was a saddened Victorian, topped off by a clock tower. They probably intended to have a real clock but the money must have run short, so there was nothing but a painted face on which painted hands stolidly proclaimed the hour of 6 P.M.—or 6 A.M., according to how you felt—until the thing was torn down. At that, it was a welcome change from the monotonous 8:18 of the watchmakers' signs.

Louvred doors swung back and forth on seldom idle hinges in front of the city's myriad saloons. There was the *North Pole*, and the *First and Last Chance*, and the *Snug Harbor* and *The Telephone*. *The Telephone* was an object of interest even to the very young, for it sported, bolted to its clapboard front, a huge wooden telephone which could be depended upon to catch the eye. It was a telephone complete with google-eye bells, a long-necked transmitter, and even the crank on the side. Such instruments were common in the outlands. It was the heyday of the party line when everyone knew everyone's business. The little telephone exchange was, of course, operated by "hello girls"—the automatic telephone, depending at times vainly upon the intelligence of the subscriber, was too far in the dim future to be a cause of worry. Telegraph service was limited and there were times when the long rows of bluish-green "crowfoot" batteries in the back room of the little office down on F Street were barely able to keep the spark of life in the thin wire leading to Los Angeles.

Local nimrods found quail and rabbit plentiful around Spreckels Heights and University Heights, but had to content themselves with this sort of game alone; narrow-minded city aldermen had passed an ordinance which forbade the shooting of deer in the city limits. Such is the penalty of progress.

Tall clipper ships sailed in with their cargoes, and deepwater men thronged the lower reaches of the town. Labor difficulties came. There were sluggings and shootings; the *Otago* was blown up, and a gang raided the British bark *Darra*, dragging members of her crew ashore. The men were British subjects, and a threatened call by one of Her Majesty's warships finally brought the place to its senses. The *Itata* affair broke, and put San Diego into the datelines of press dispatches throughout the world, as the interned ship was stolen by her crew and headed for Chile, with the old U.S.S. *Charleston* puffing along in hot pursuit and a fog of soft-coal smoke.

There came a time when drought added its parching breath to the trials of the little town, and the level of the water in the sands of the San Diego River bed dropped steadily. The water was pumped to a standpipe which arose like a thin black obelisk from Spreckels Heights and equalized the pressure throughout the town, but did nothing to improve the quality of the fluid; the receding water still left rings of alkali around the edges of the china washbasins. Lawns and gardens could be watered only at certain hours of the day, and strictly by hand. If the hose was laid down even for a moment, the penalty was the capping of all outside faucets, and many were the lawns which became yellow and dead during those dry months—and years.

The Spanish War came, and the naval battalion of the local militia manned the asthmatic old gunboat *Pinta*, waiting for the battle orders which never came.

Some unknown public enemy invented the gasoline cook stove, and much entertainment for curious crowds resulted therefrom. A deep-throated whistle, blowing the code number of whichever fire alarm box was pulled, advertised to the town just where they should go. Teams of plunging horses dragged the tooting clanging old "steamers" to the scene of the blaze, with spindly-wheeled hose carts and a lumbering, homemade hook-and-ladder in their wake. There were some wonderful fires, among which that of the Dew Drop Inn still stands out. The Dew Drop Inn was a place of plebeian entertainment, and its passing to a fiery beyond was not without incident. Firemen toiled valiantly and finally saved the barroom ice box, which arose like a disreputable phoenix from among the steaming embers. Firemen in those days were not the abstemious crew that they are today, and a raid on the ice box was in order. Dawn found hose carts full of singers trailing back to the fire houses. The outfit at Second and E Streets had a jovial foreman, and a jovial driver. At 5 A.M. they conferred:

"You're drunk," said the foreman, "And I'm going to harness up the hose cart and drive you home."

"No," replied the offended driver, "I'm not drunk; it's you that's drunk, and I'm going to drive *you* home."

"I know," said the foreman, brightening up, "Let's drive each other home!"

So once more they harnessed up the team—two radical cayuses, only recently broken to double harness. Two blocks from the engine houses they went up onto a sidewalk and upset, the overturned hose cart resting firmly on the driver's chest. He was extricated, unhurt but greatly sobered. Both he and the foreman knew that the chief, a profane old gentleman, would hear of it any minute now, and they began to plan their alibi. It was decided that the team had shied, and that when they tried to pull them back into the street, the rein had broken. In support of this theory, the foreman solemnly drew his jack-knife, cut the stitches at a joint in the rein, and pulled it apart. About that time the chief drove up and asked questions—rather embarrassing questions. The foreman made his speech, and produced the two ends of the rein as Exhibit A for the defense. The chief looked at the rein with some interest.

"A good story," he growled, "A dam' good story. Only—*you so-and-sos cut the wrong rein!*"

But going to fires was not the town's sole amusement. You could hire a tally-ho and drive out for a day in the country, or pack up your lunch and visit the old lighthouse on top of Point Loma. In those days, it was just "the old lighthouse," and its American origin was known and respected. It was years later that some zealot decided that its building by American army engineers, as the first lighthouse in Southern California, lacked sufficient romantic interest, and hung on the defenseless landmark the title which it bears today—"The Old Spanish Lighthouse."

On Sundays the fishing fleet would be in port, and if you wanted a little real sport you could charter one of the tricky little double-ended sloops and go out for a race. There wasn't much difference in hull and rig between fishing boats and yachts in those days, and there were some lively contests.

An asthmatic, walking-beam ferryboat, the *Benicia,* worked with her more modern but equally wheezy teammate, the *Coronado,* to give access to the sprawling little village of Coronado, over across the bay. Trans-bay travel in those days was something of a sporting proposition; if you got on the *Benicia,* it was touch and go whether you would land in Coronado, at National City, or somewhere in the lower bay. The *Benicia* suffered from frequent misery among her machinery, and it was not altogether unusual for a puffing tug to go out and capture her when she got tired of her prosaic run and decided to go where the tide willed.

North Island was a tawny sea of brush, and boasted but one inhabitant—the ancient mariner who tended the clanking marine railway which was in those days the only place in Southern California where a ship of any size could be drydocked. The place teemed with rabbits —you could go there any night, set a lantern down in a clear spot and retire to the seclusion of a bush to await developments. Your wait would not be long; about fifteen feet from the light two upstanding ears would appear. Then would come two more, then others. In a little while there would be a regular picket fence of furry ears in a circle around the lantern. Then you could do as your conscience dictated, with rifle or slingshot.

Brickyard Cove, down the Coronado sandpit, shared with North Island the popularity of picnic places, and many a Sunday saw the little anchorage crowded with long-sparred sloops, fat catboats and slim sharpies. Sometimes the womenfolk came along; other times the affairs were strictly stag, with a jovial crowd gathering around the keg and sailing home, full of brew and music, as the sun was sinking toward Point Loma.

Single-trucked trolley cars extended their frail tracks to Logan Heights, to Golden Hill, and through sparsely settled University Heights to Mission Cliff Gardens and The Pavillion. Here you could amuse yourself by looking at the caged canaries, or by riding the merry-go-round, or by visiting the Camera Obscura to stand in awed delight in the darkened, octagonal room, while a slowly revolving mirror cast onto an oilcloth-topped table a picture of Mission Valley in colors which seemed unnaturally bright and more than a little gaudy.

The double-decked streetcar came and was a nine days' wonder. You could climb the winding stair behind the motorman to the long seats on top, under their flat wooden canopy, and look down in scorn on the surreys and drays and hacks which drove along the dusty streets. Over in Coronado, street cars towed long, open, cross-seated trailers down to Tent City, the new resort on the beach. There you could spend the day in getting sunburned, and the evening in sitting on hard benches to listen to Ohlmeyer's Band playing from a concave music shell up over the café. If you were sufficiently old and sinful you could retire to the *Royal Inn,* Coronado's one and only saloon, for amusement of a more blasé nature. If you had a week or so on your hands you could rent a tent with delirium-tremens stripes, unpack your bathing suit and toothbrush and nightie, and nestle down to the companionship of the sand flies. Ah, those were the happy days!

Dinky, open railway cars, pulled by locomotives with bob-tailed tenders, balloon-topped smokestacks and huge water tanks on top of their boilers, formed the passenger rolling stock of the old National City & Otay Railway. They provided rapid transit—of a sort—for the commuters from the towns to the south of San Diego, and bore tourists to the American side of the line at Tijuana. Here you boarded a stage and, under the direction of old Reuben the Guide, spent what the circulars described as "two delightful hours in quaint old Mexico." There was a regular formula for the Tijuana visit, in those days; Papa bought some black cigars at Jorge Ibs' store, Mama bought a plate or a cup and saucer edged in red, white and green, the children were decked out with straw sombreros, and all hands sent back postcards "from abroad." Tijuana, with its single street of one-story frame buildings and its kerosene lampposts, was a vastly different place from the Tijuana of today. On the way back, the train stopped for water in a convenient olive grove, where unwary tourists were prevailed upon to alight and enjoy the pleasures of eating olives which they themselves picked. They never did it a second time.

La Jolla, where you went to see the caves and the sea lions, was reached by a diminutive steam train scarcely as long as its own name—*the Los Angeles & San Diego Beach Railway*—which had hopes someday of reaching Los Angeles, but never did. The San Diego, Cuyamaca & Eastern ran out through La Mesa, El Cajon, Santee and Lakeside to Foster, where the hardier travelers boarded a stagecoach for the long pull up the mountain grades to Ramona and the rest of the real back country. At Lakeside was a racetrack and a big hotel. The latter was an example of mid-Victorian architecture gone berserk, but it boasted a chef who was one in a million. For a ridiculously low figure you could go there and eat yourself into a stupor that would last three days.

Naphtha launches now were replacing sailboats on the bay, and grotesque, consumptive automobiles were appearing. The Diamond and the Alta and the other livery stables were beginning to feel the competition of motor-car barns, which were known as "garridges." The old bandstand in the Plaza was torn down. Ships crossing skysail yards became a rarity. Electric signs began to appear, and dusty streets were paved. A Rambler touring car, its tonneau rebuilt into a hose body, became the first motor fire engine. The town was becoming a city.

(1934)

The Cable Cars of San Diego

Jerry MacMullen

When Kipling delved into California lore to emerge with his delightful yarn called "The Bow Flume Cable-Car," was he drawing on his memory of Victorian transportation in San Francisco—or did he have San Diego in mind?

There is a question to set tongues a-wagging, and to start drawing room—and tap room—discussions along the lines of "Whose cable car was it, anyhow?"

Kipling's funicular railway, the brainchild of a mechanically-minded bartender named Howling O'-Grady, of the mythical town of Bow Flume, certainly had much in common with San Diego's cable cars. Not only were there various novelties in the manner of how the grip engaged the cable, but the car itself was, in its far from quiet way, a thing of exotic beauty. And the cable system of San Diego further resembled that of Bow Flume in that it was, like the rocket, gorgeous but of short duration.

The San Diego cars were maroon and gray, and had white roofs set off with stained-glass windows. There were nickel-plated grab rails, the lettering on the cars was so ornate as to be a bit difficult to read, and the cars weren't numbered—they were named, like Pullmans. You might, for instance, ride out to Mission Cliff gardens in the car *Las Penasquitas*, or go downtown for a shopping trip aboard the *Cuyamaca*—to return in *El Escondido* or *La Jolla* or the *San Juan Capistrano*.

It was back in 1889 that San Diego decided to have a cable car system. . . .

By the late spring of 1890, all was in readiness, and at 10 A.M. June 7, *El Escondido* headed downtown from the powerhouse. . . . The first paying passenger was a woman whose name became known and revered by horticulturists and nature lovers throughout the west, the late Miss Kate Sessions.

It was that afternoon, however, that San Diego went cable-happy in a big way. In honor of the occasion, *El Escondido* was all but hidden in palm branches and flowers, and had aboard the famous old City Guard Band. They started up from the foot of Sixth Street and over C to Fourth, where the *San Juan Capistrano*—which followed them—picked up the official party. There was some delay while Mayor Douglas made an extensive and florid speech. You know—one of those jobs in which the speaker points with pride, puts his shoulder to the wheel, waves the flag, and all that. It made everyone very happy, in the best Victorian manner. . . . Then Governor R. W. Waterman and his party, who had come out from the old Brewster Hotel, joined with the mayor and other dignitaries aboard the *San Juan Capistrano* and jingled merrily out to Mission Cliff Gardens, while the band played on. . . .

And so the line rumbled on. Those two Corliss engines spun quietly and efficiently inside the powerhouse; there was a cheerful plume of coal smoke from the tall brick smokestack at Fourth and Spruce, and the glittering little fleet of cable cars went up and down the hill and out to the edge of Mission Valley. There were, of course, some minor flaws, such as *Montezuma* being a minute late, and thus holding up *San Ysidora* on the siding at Normal and El Cajon avenues, or *Tia Juana* scaring the wits out of a team of horses pulling a surrey from the Alta Stables. And there was the regrettable incident of the powerhouse turntable which someone left set the wrong way and *Alvarado*—or was it *Point Loma?*—fell in. Yet no one ever had his person or his feelings hurt by one of those cars, and San Diego really loved them.

But all the while, the skies were turning gray, and the cold wind of economic unrest was growing in force. As the autumn wind brings the soft rustle of scurrying leaves, so did this wind bring rustlings of another, and more ominous, nature—the soft rustle of banks, one by one, folding up. Came at last that grim morning when gloomy depositors stood in line before the locked doors of the bank which had been the principal backers of the cable cars. With its passing, so also passed the San Diego Cable Railway, at the ripe old age of thirteen months. The Citizen's Traction Company bought up the franchises and equipment and, apparently having the good will of a more durable bank, electrified the system. The cables were pulled up and the powerhouse was pulled down, leaving only gaunt masonry footings in the canyon at Fourth and Spruce. Forlorn and alone, *Cuyamaca* and *Montezuma*—which had not been modernized—stood for years on an abandoned spur, and the stones and sling-shots of neighborhood brats slowly reduced them to splintered wreckage.

And so ended a brief but colorful episode in Southern California transportation. San Francisco reigns today as the undisputed cable car capital of the world, her citizens having, so far, had sense enough to retain the quaint system not only as a means of getting from here to there, but also as a tourist attraction of worldwide note.

(1947)

Low Life in '88

Jerry MacMullen

San Diego, by the end of '88, boasted sixty-four retail and three wholesale groceries. The liquid side of the citizenry's sustenance was not overlooked, however, for we find that, at the same time, there were seventy-one saloons and twelve houses which dealt in liquor in case lots. Names of some of the joints were not without color: there was the Tub o' Blood, the Silver Moon, Rosario Hall, the Yankee Doodle, the Pacific Squadron and a host of others. Untrammeled recreation of other sorts was far from lacking, and what went on beneath the bespangled chandeliers of the Turf, Canary Cottage and a number of others was a subject over which a discreet veil of secrecy was drawn in polite society. Newspaper crusading was present then as now, and the same journal which gravely rebuked the steamship company for running its steam cars at too high a speed to be consistent with the temperament of dray teams in the vicinity paused a few days later to state that "No man can pass along the streets without being hallooed at by the shameless women." Tsk, tsk, tsk!

(1932)

San Diego Unaffected by War in Mexico

Though San Diego is the largest city on the Mexican-Yankee line, wars and rumors of wars in Mexico have affected it about as much as if it were located on the Canadian line. Business and social life goes on just as if there were no turmoil below the imaginary line. Only the arrival of the regular steamers with refugees from the Mexican ports south of the line remind that there are troubles down in that "poco tiempo" country.

As a matter of fact San Diego is too busy building wharves, docks, piers, enlarging her harbor facilities, water system, streets and her business blocks, to say nothing of her big Panama-California Exposition to pay any attention to rumors from the southern republic.

Mexican and Central American steamers have arrived and departed on regular schedules ever since the first outbreak of trouble in Mexico three years ago. The only possible difference these troubles can make in San Diego is to deprive the exposition of a Mexican exhibit and this is not a conclusion yet. . . .

San Diego, though only fourteen miles from the Mexican border, probably is less affected by the "Mexican situation" than any other city on the entire international border line and, judging from the increase in bank clearings and building permits, is less affected by the "financial situation" than any other city in the country.

(1913)

1919: Boosterism on Broadway

San Diego County has something to sell, and it is not going to be bashful about announcing the fact to the world. Its salesmen will be the leading businessmen of the city, its market will be the great middle-west and its medium of exchange will be the San Diego-California Club, the membership of which is composed of the "salesmen" who are putting San Diego County on the market.

Having something to sell, it is only logical to suppose that a county would endeavor to find a market and then put the matter before the public. That is exactly what San Diego has decided to do, again setting an active example to Southern California counties as progressive as that of passing the first bond issue for good roads almost fifteen years ago.

In view of the fact that the thing San Diego has to sell is "a place to live," it is only natural that those who go to make up the personnel of the San Diego-California Club are the men who have been prominent in the development of the city as a liveable place, and they are self-appointed as a reception committee to meet and help the incoming home builder.

But let the officers of the "new idea" club, which is vitally interested for its modernity, speak for themselves, from the pages of their prospectus:

"We will maintain permanent headquarters and a standing reception committee. This committee will be paid men of such ability and personality as will make it a pleasure to the stranger to meet them; men who will make him feel the spirit of our welcome.

"Every newcomer will be met personally by one of

these committeemen, who will sit down with him and get acquainted, learn what his interests have been and what his desires are, and then acquaint him with the conditions as they actually are in San Diego. And before he has finished, he will give the newcomer a list of half a dozen or so names of local club members, businessmen or others whose ideas and tastes are the same as those of the newcomers. He will be told to call upon these gentlemen and that he will enjoy meeting them.

"After the party has gone, the committeemen will call up these individuals and tell them of his arrival, where he is stopping, and of the fact that his interests are along the same general lines as those of our home citizen, and that it will be a pleasure as well as a benefit to the community for our local men to communicate with him, to call and make him feel at home. This work divided among several hundred members will not be an imposition on any of us, and it will be productive of tremendous results.

"The newcomer or honorary club member will be instructed to use his honorary club membership card wherever he goes, and display it when going into a store or business house, and he will find that upon using it he will receive the same courteous treatment that would be accorded to him had he been a resident of San Diego for the past fifteen years.

"When a local club member sees one of these cards, he or she will realize that here is a man whom the club has paid to bring to San Diego; that it is a duty and a pleasure to encourage him to stay here. Before the newcomer has been a week in San Diego, he will feel at home.

"A part of the work of this organization will be to get, first, the proprietors of all stores and hotels, and second, the clerks of all such establishments into the spirit of this reception. The organization will get together occasionally at some function or informal ball, a trip to the Morena Dam, and the mountains, or possibly for a day of sports on the bay. The object being to revive local interest in the pleasurable things for which we have such wonderful opportunities in San Diego, and to get our people back into the spirit of the joy of living, so that when our new friends come they will feel this spirit from every angle.

"This work will start as soon as our subscriptions are in, and it will go on while we are advertising in the East, so that when these people begin to arrive here, we will be in a spirit to receive them."

(1919)

Old Town, Spring of 1940

Henry Berrey

Old Town, California's oldest community, plans to gather all its historic background together and put on an authentic, dyed-in-the-wool fiesta on June 15 and 16. Old Town is three or four miles north of San Diego and is the original site of the city. The plaza in the middle of Old Town could be called the Plymouth Rock of California for it was here in 1769 that California first became an entity. Here also, skirmishes of considerable importance took place between the Mexican and American armies back in the days of the conquest.

The fiesta will be like most fiestas, with horses and music and señoritas, but there will be an unmistakable feeling of reality surrounding the fripperies of the show. The old Estudillo house will probably be one of the centers of attraction. A great deal went on here in the old days. The Estudillos were a wealthy family and on occasions loaned their home for a church, an orphanage and a school. What's more, Ramona and Allessandro were married here.

Old Town is worth a lot of poking around. . . .

(1940)

San Diego—A California City
reviewed by Carey McWilliams

A recent publication of the Federal Writers Project in California is *San Diego—A California City*. The volume is part of the American Guide Series which constitutes, of course, the major work upon which writers have been engaged since the inception of the project. As a guide book the volume on San Diego is both interesting and informative, being replete with maps, references and directions. The historical material, of which there is a great deal, is rather fragmentary but it does contain a readable account of the rise of San Diego.

The miscellaneous information to be found in the book should enable San Diegans to add spice and zest to dinnertable gossip about their interesting community. It will enable them, for example, to tell the incredulous Eastern cousin that, on the average, less than nine days in the year in San Diego are without sunshine; and to balance this profound observation with the staggering announcement that the largest blue topaz in the world was discovered near San Diego and that the neighboring mountains have yielded such esoteric gems as kunzite and tourmaline and more than a hundred other "semiprecious stones."

It is diverting, also, to learn that the aborigines of the region believed in a powerful deity with the attractive name of Chinigchinich; that they attributed magical properties to the skin of the bear; and that they loved to feast on whalemeat and smear themselves from head to foot with "rancid whale blubber."

Those finicky souls who are forever complaining of the encroachment of Los Angeles upon other communities should be silenced with the reminder that San Diego was once administered as a department of Los Angeles. This vindicates Angelenos of avarice: they have relinquished sovereignty, not hogged it.

Many were the curious happenings recorded in the *San Diego Herald* (founded in 1851). In 1852 the county clerk was deputized to take over the functions of all county offices, his colleagues having decided to attend a prolonged and joyous fiesta. Outlawry in the murky past of this sunshine-flooded community was quite general; so general, in fact, that the death penalty was inflicted for all thefts over $50 in value. The *Herald* reported on one occasion that "a lot of greasers had a *baile* the other evening and stoned a poor Indian until he quietly laid down and died."

In 1887 San Diego witnessed what is perhaps the most astonishing boom in the history of California real estate speculation. Within a few months, the population rose to 40,000, lizards and sand giving way to jerry-built houses and wharves. When the crash came in 1888, the city was virtually abandoned. Ten thousand people left in a few months. By 1890 the population stood at about 17,000. In 1872 the community had three stores and twenty-three saloons.

The chapter on the cultural attainments of the region is rather disappointing. The compilers did their best to make an impressive record, but the material was apparently not very promising. From a literary point of view, mention is made of Max Miller and Harold Bell Wright and of *Zoonooz*, a magazine issued by the San Diego Zoological Society. More might have been said. In North San Diego, for example, resides Edith Summers Kelley, who wrote a distinguished first novel, *Weeds*, and who was once secretary to Upton Sinclair at Halcyon Hall. And the authors fail to mention one of the best pieces ever written about San Diego: a chapter by Edmund Wilson in *The American Jitters*.

Aside from these unimportant omissions, the volume, which may be purchased for fifty cents, is an excellent piece of work.

(1939)

Wartime San Diego—
A Personal Postscript

Jack Smith

The war began and ended for me in San Diego. There was a middle, of course, but that is best forgotten. For most of us, men and women, the memories that stay vivid are of cities—Washington, San Francisco, Honolulu. . . .

The alien swamps and plains and hilltops grow dark on the landscape of nostalgia.

We see only the gaudy neons in the streets, hear only the songs of the jukeboxes . . . *"Small Hotel"* . . . *"I'll Be Seeing You"* . *"Long Ago and Far Away."*

At the height of World War II San Diego was one big jukebox, lighted up and blaring out.

Like hundreds of thousands of other young men, I

first saw wartime San Diego from a train I was a Marine Corps recruit. The train rolled into the old Santa Fe station at the foot of Broadway and disgorged us— a thousand recruits of every stamp, each to be swallowed up by this hungry city, for a thousand separate fates.

The Santa Fe depot was the closest I came to the fleshpots of wartime San Diego for the next eight weeks. A bus snatched me and my fellow Marine recruits off the platform and trundled us off to purgatory.

The Marine Corps recruit depot was then, and is today, a vast mud flat created in North San Diego Bay by dredges. It is covered by lawns and huge patches of concrete and asphalt called parade grounds. But it remains a mud flat.

The bus took us through the gate and dropped us off at a point distinguished only by the presence of a grizzled, potbellied master sergeant with a face like an old tomato. As we streamed off the bus we heard a low rumbling sound and saw that this old bloat's enormous belly was in motion. We realized he was laughing.

He lined us up and waddled up and down the line, looking us over, shaking his head slowly, regarding us with an expression of disbelief and Falstaffian outrage.

Somehow, I sensed, this improbable monster was my superior. I was in his charge.

I looked past him and saw the San Diego skyline and the lovely green and brown hills with their confetti of houses. And at that moment, for me, the war began.

Later on in the war I sometimes saw prisoners-of-war who were *in* but not *of* the place where they were held. I knew how they felt. I had spent eight weeks like that in San Diego.

I don't suggest that it is contrived, but it is surely an incidental frustration of life at boot camp that all the days of one's captivity are spent within sight of gleaming structures that are the very symbols of freedom, not to mention wine, women and song.

In the weeks that followed there was one word that became foremost in the minds of us all. An obsession; a shibboleth. It was *liberty*. It was not liberty in the sense of what we were fighting for, the freedom of all peoples everywhere. It was not the *liberté* of the Revolution. No, it was more immediate and vital and personal than those noble concepts.

It was hardly more than a rumor, actually. It was the liberty we were going to get in *San Diego* after we had graduated from boot camp and been readmitted to society.

I cannot remember now whether in fact this impossible dream was ever realized for all of us. I doubt it. I think most were given another look at Broadway from the Santa Fe station and rushed on to our appointed posts.

I was luckier. I was stamped for public relations duty in the Marine Air Corps and given a short bus ride to my new post at North Island Naval Air Station. North Island is so called because it is the northern end of Coronado Island, which lies in the bay just across from boot camp.

As the seagull flies, I had traveled only a mile or two. But it was another world. After a brief quarantine, I was given liberty.

In those days there was only one way to get from North Island to San Diego. That was by the ferry boat; unless one had access to the captain's gig. The ferry cost a nickel and was naturally called the "nickel snatcher." It was a creaky old tub, but to a man on his first liberty it was Cleopatra's barge.

When on liberty in wartime San Diego the proper thing to do was to fling oneself into manhood as quickly as possible by visiting the bars that erupted along Broadway and its sidestreets all the way from the waterfront to Horton's Plaza. This was a rite much like the puberty rites of primitive peoples, and was not completed until the apprentice had visited every last station on the route and reached a state of levitation.

This was not to say that downtown San Diego was wicked. It was well policed by the locals and the Shore Patrol, whose avoidance, of course, was a requirement of the ritual.

By grace of the laws of California, every bar in town went dark and quiet at midnight. I doubt if any wartime law was more ruthlessly enforced. Also, no matter what the Marine Corps said, you were not a man till you were twenty-one.

Each of these establishments employed a young woman, often toothsome but always inflexible, who stood at the door and demanded to inspect the ID card of every fighting man who looked as if he might not yet have entered manhood in the eyes of the State of California.

One of the reasons I visited so many bars, I now realize, was the pleasure I got out of being momentarily thwarted by one of these incorruptible Lorelei and asked for my *bona fides*. I suppose I enjoyed this repeated reassurance that while I was actually over twenty-one I still looked young.

San Diego was something more, of course, than a long dim bar filled like a cattle car with disenchanted men looking into their beers or ogling unattainable B-girls or braying songs such as *"Bless 'em All"* or *"Pistol Packin' Mama"* or, God help us, one of the numerous national anthems of Texas.

Through all the hours we spent watering our withered psyches, waiting for our call to higher missions out there, enormous energies were being expended all about us.

The great aircraft plants swarmed like termitaries

with workers, men and women, who labored round the clock, in three shifts, over airframes that would soon be in combat.

Day and night these artisans clogged the streets and cafés and houses and apartments and hotel rooms, and pursued their revels away from the downtown oases of servicemen.

Day and night the fruits of their labors screamed and thundered in the skies above us, and every hour a new one was born full-fledged.

Day and night the destroyers and submarines and carriers slipped in and out of the harbor, gray against gray, like skulking cats at twilight. We saw them and knew vaguely that something was going on somewhere far away, and somebody was tending to it.

Not all my liberty was drowned in the parlors of lower Broadway. The NCO in charge of my public relations unit, a staff sergeant and a man of the world, introduced me into the *haut monde* of San Diego.

Sergeant Krisco, let us call him, was immune to the vulgar temptations of lower Broadway. He would disembark from the nickel snatcher like an admiral and walk all the way, past every garish trap, to the stately U. S. Grant Hotel, where, by means of which to this day I have no knowledge, he maintained a private room.

Sergeant Krisco taught me to go first class. Thus it was that I began to frequent the bar of the U. S. Grant and the Sky Room of the El Cortez. Once, incredibly, I even found myself in the grand saloon of the Coronado Hotel, the very inner fortress of Officer Country.

On that occasion, which burns more vividly in my memory than even my disheartening arrival at boot camp, Sergeant Krisco and I occupied a table next to one occupied by a lieutenant colonel, a full colonel and a major general. There is no question in my mind about those ranks. They are as unfaded as the Boy Scout Oath.

At one point, when Sergeant Krisco was reminiscing about the perils of life as a Hollywood studio publicity man, I suddenly became aware that the major general, whose chair was nearest our table, was listening to Sergeant Krisco, not the colonel! I realized then that clothes and emblems do not make the reconteur.

Sergeant Krisco's path and mine were to cross several more times during the war, here and there along the West Coast and in the Pacific. I never saw him looking anything but *distingué*. He never lost his aplomb, and he always had a jeep, and sometimes a fairly attractive girl.

One day, inevitably, orders came and I was gone before I could pack. That was the way of the Corps. You were never given time to pack everything, so that always something had to be left behind. These objects, usually priceless, were routinely confiscated, I suppose, by the top sergeant.

The war was over when I came back.

This time it was by sea. We were on a small escort carrier. She carried no planes. Her mission was to bring home the weary and the hopeful for repatriation, love and happiness, all the enemies of man, everywhere, having been put down.

Hours before landfall we were all up on the flight deck, our eyes straining at the horizon.

Then the hazy low lump of hills rose above the morning sea, and then the first structures, and finally the whole wonderful patchwork, like a Cezanne canvas.

There were shouts of "There she is!" and "Home!" or simple, speechless, exultant outcries.

My heart began to swell and thump a bit. My spine shivered. My palms grew moist.

But intellectually I remained cool. It was not San

Diego to me until I could positively identify the Sky Room of the El Cortez.

There was a band waiting on the wharf, and that cherished symbol of what we had been fighting for, a majorette, her blonde curls bouncing and her plump legs flashing in the San Diego sun.

As we filed down the gangway every man of us imagined himself a hero, and some were.

Two days later, at twilight, which was not by accident, I sat at a table by the window of the Sky Room. My wife was sitting across from me. She had come down on the train, the train which had been the lifeline of the war in Southern California.

The night fell and the lights winked on. The city below us had exhausted itself. It had labored mightily and was done. It seemed to be lying there, breathing hard, like a spent fighter.

I was filled with an unimaginable joy. It was all over; and it would never happen again.

"Long ago and far away. . . ."

(1969)

II
Enter the Motor Car

———— ❦ ◆❯ ❦ ————

In its early years Touring Topics *was devoted* almost exclusively to the immediate concerns of the motor car owner in Southern California. Car owners then were still a fairly exclusive and intimate breed and they shared interests and displayed loyalties which in these jaded times might seem excessive. Some of the challenges (and even dangers) facing the early-day motorists make pleasantly nostalgic reading today. Hardly anyone nowadays gets "lost" in a car, and a dirt road is hard to find. A trip to San Diego, whether by "the coast route" or "the inland route" was then an uncertain undertaking. But the successful completion of such a trip, and the wonderful discoveries made along the way, were cause for uninhibited rejoicing.

Sign Posters

The City Council of San Diego has contributed $125.00 and her two most prominent citizens have added $100.00 each to a fund to be used in posting road signs throughout the city.

Many motorists frequently find it difficult to find the proper avenues leading from the city to the main country thoroughfares, but after these signs are properly erected, no difficulty will be experienced along this line in San Diego. The Automobile Club of Southern California, working in conjunction with the San Diego Advisory Board, are now preparing signs for posting the Coast line between Los Angeles and San Diego. While this route is now practically impassable owing to the recent rains, it will, when properly posted, be one of the most picturesque runs in Southern California.

(1909)

Sign Molesters

Word has been received that a number of road signs erected by the Automobile Club of Southern California, on the main highway between Rainbow and Bonsall, and between Temecula and Bonsall, have been badly tampered with and in some instances the posts have been completely broken off.

For the information of those who may be able to furnish data sufficient to lead to the arrest and conviction of these miscreants, we wish to state that a permanent reward of $200.00 is offered for the arrest and conviction of anyone defacing these signs.

While on this subject, it may be well to mention that a reward is standing ready to be paid to the party furnishing information leading to the arrest and conviction of any person or persons stealing an automobile or any article from an automobile, belonging to a member of the Club.

(1909)

District Attorney Says "Stop!"

Word has come from San Diego that the District Attorney has determined that fast racing between Los Angeles and San Diego must stop. He is said to have deputized a number of farmers, residing along the route of travel, and instructed them to keep a watchful eye on speeding motorists. It is believed to be the ultimate aim of this movement to do away with the record breaking speed such as recently developed by the Franklin and the Rambler cars.

(1909)

Social Notes

The new addition to the Hotel del Coronado garage, which was planned large enough to handle any possible increase in the business this winter, was filled to overflowing before the end of January and the garage's rent cars had to be moved out to make room for touring parties making the hotel their headquarters while seeing the "back country" and their many trips into old Mexico.

The automobile has added one more asset to the wealth of Southern California. The value of "climate" to this part of the state has never been questioned, but we hardly appreciate, at the present, the value of the natural beauty of the South Coast as an important factor in the lengthening of the winter season at both ends; our Eastern friends who bring their cars come earlier in the season than formerly and remain until later in the season before starting north along the coast, as they wish to ensure pleasant weather for their trip.

Full credit must be given to the automobile for this change, as it is only by means of the auto that the innumerable points of interest may be visited with ease and without loss of time. This year the season will last until late in April, many of the regular winter residents of Coronado preferring a longer visit here to taking chances of arriving in the north with their cars before the late spring cold snaps are over.

Auto parties making the trip from Los Angeles to Coronado should notify the hotel of the time of their arrival as the Hotel del Coronado is now "packed to the limit" and suitable accommodations for large parties should be secured by advance notice, so the management can arrange to have rooms close together, and not scatter the party all over the house in whatever rooms may be at their disposal. The indications are that the house will be full until late in April this year, so it would be well for all motorists to bear this in mind.

Mr. F. J. Mackey, the noted polo enthusiast, motored down the coast, arriving here Thursday, and will remain here until after the Polo Tournament, which will end March 29th.

Mr. and Mrs. William Wrigley, Jr., of Chicago, accompanied by Mrs. Clara Albright, motored down from Los Angeles and will see all the points of interest in Southern California before returning east. Mr. Wrigley is the president of the American Chicle Co.

Mr. H. M. Byllesby, who winters at Coronado regularly, has arrived with his family for an extended stay, and shipped his car directly to Coronado. He will enjoy the beauties of the San Diego "back country" for a couple of months and leave the explorations of the regions farther north until later in the year.

Mrs. J. A. Graves and J. A. Graves, Jr., came down from Los Angeles in their motor to spend the weekend.

Mr. and Mrs. Nat. C. Goodwin and party of friends also made the trip to Coronado in autos and remained here several days longer than they intended as they found many points of interest worth seeing before returning home.

Col. and Mrs. Lambert of Chicago, accompanied by Mr. and Mrs. B. H. Conkling, motored down to Coronado, arriving on Saturday—and reported an exceptionally pleasant trip.

One of the parties who came down last week report having been lost in the mountains and going up to Pala, and express great pleasure at having done so, as they claim to have visited the most beautiful scenery they had ever seen during their motoring experiences.

(1910)

"A Jolly Party"

San Diego County is becoming the mecca of autoists and many delightful drives are found there among the hills and mountains as well as an eighty-mile drive along the coast in view of the ocean.

A jolly party of twenty people in three machines owned by S. P. Fay of the Fay Fruit Company, O. T. Johnson and P. M. Johnson, all prominent citizens of Los Angeles, and their families, have just recently returned from a four days' trip, more than delighted with what they have seen and enthusiastic boosters for our most southern section of California.

Starting from Los Angeles Tuesday, April 26, [1910] the day's run was via Riverside, Elsinore, Temecula, Oceanside to Stratford Inn at Del Mar, the distance being 147 miles, the roads on the whole being good and the party made the trip with comfort.

On Wednesday morning, under the guidance of Col. Ed Fletcher, the party left Stratford Inn at 10 o'clock for San Diego, via the famous Torrey Pines boulevard through La Jolla, thence to Point Loma and Ocean Beach over the magnificent speedway recently constructed. A short visit to Coronado and the hotel was made and then a run through the city of San Diego, viewing the points of interest.

At 2:30 P.M. the entire party started for Cuyamaca Lake, sixty miles away, a mile high and tucked in among the pines in the Cuyamaca mountains, where Col.

Fletcher had promised a fish dinner of bass from the lake. A short stop was made at the famous Grossmont Park, where a number of celebrities of this country will be located, including Mme. Schumann-Heink, Mme. Teresa Carreno, Carrie Jacobs Bond, John Vance Cheney, Owen Wister and many others. . . . From Grossmont a delightful run was made through El Cajon Valley. The road via Alpine and Descanso was through a succession of beautiful hills and valleys, magnificent oaks and sycamores, rocky hillsides and rugged canyons for the entire distance until the timber line of pine was reached above Descanso. A short spin of twelve miles was then made through heavy pine and oak timber, while every once in a while a live mountain stream was crossed with beautiful fern brakes bordering same, giving the New Englander a taste of his mother country.

Cuyamaca Lake was reached at 7 P.M. and seventy fish, caught that afternoon in the lake, met a sad fate. There is no more beautiful spot in California than Cuyamaca Lake, nearly two miles in length and one-half to one mile in width, "tucked in," as it were, among the mountains, and from whose depth a beautiful wooded island arises. Some day when railway transportation is furnished, Cuyamaca Lake will be Southern California's most famous resort. The ladies were taught how to catch fish from the lake and they were so plentiful that the stories are unbelievable.

Leaving Cuyamaca Lake at 8:30 Thursday morning, the way still led through heavy timber towards Julian. At one point on the Cuyamaca road a magnificent panorama is secured of Lost Valley, Salton Sea, Colorado desert and the mountains of Arizona, a sight which when once seen is never forgotten. Julian was reached at 9:30, where a short stop was made for gasoline.

From there the road to Pine Hills, two miles away,

was a rugged tract of mountain timber land, wild and picturesque. . . .

After a short, enjoyable walk through the forest of pine and oak, over a mountain stream via a rustic log bridge, the machines were again entered and the run made via Wynola through the famous apple country down Santa Ysabel grade and across the Santa Ysabel ranch. From here the road led through beautiful oaks, an interesting Indian reservation, thence down and across the famous Warner ranch. At 11:30 the Mesa Grande grade was reached. . . .

Continuing through the Mesa Grande Indian Reservation to Mesa Grande proper, a short and interesting visit was made to the magnificent cherry orchard of genial Ed Davis, where we feasted on early cherries.

Leaving Mesa Grande at 12:00, we went down through beautiful canyons and over rolling hills to Ramona, a distance of fifteen miles, where a plain but well cooked luncheon was secured from everybody's friend, Mrs. Kearney.

Leaving Ramona at 2:30, an afternoon run was made to Del Mar via Poway grade, a beautiful, rugged trip through the mountains, thence over the Poway Hills on the E. W. Scripps famous boulevard to Miramar, past Mr. Scripps' home and across the Linda Vista mesa, which will some day be the most productive and healthful section of San Diego County. Del Mar was reached just before sunset. . . .

The next day the leisurely trip home was made by the coast line and the party arrived in Los Angeles early in the evening, tired but happy, having made a trip that will last for many days in the minds of those who participated.

(1910)

"This Wondrous San Diego Country . . ."

When San Diego, California, voted last year [1909], by a majority of seven to two, to create a great network of scientifically constructed roads throughout the county, at a cost of a million and a quarter of dollars, one thing of far-reaching interest was decided by that impressive victory of the progressives over the forces of near-sighted indifference—the most magnificent and delightful automobiling region in America, if not in the world, was to be opened forever. . . .

Just what these improvements in Southern California mean may be told in a few words. First of all, the climate of San Diego county—the most equable in the world—is such as to permit the automobilist to take the road at any time during the entire year. Midwinter finds the skies serene, the temperature delightful, the roadway devoid of snow or ice; midsummer—an unbroken period of balmy days and tranquil nights under Italian skies—exposes the motor traveler to nothing more annoying than a vague idea that such a continuous performance of ideal conditions cannot be true, nor last. Yet it does last. And every year is the same.

Topographically, moreover, this wondrous San Diego country lures one with half an eye for the sublime or the romantic to explore its every recess and corner. As looked down upon from the aeroplane of tomorrow, the southwesternmost county in America would present a series of foothills and mountain ranges tumbling magnificently back from the turquoise and sapphire sea, terrace above terrace, furrowed by lovely fertile valleys, dotted over with quickly-growing hamlets and towns and cities, embroidered with checkerboard orchards of orange and lemon and olive and plum, and the broad mesas and rolling uplands awaiting only the quickening touch of irrigation to burst into verdure and harvest.

From the city of San Diego, the metropolis of this Eldorado, which is fast rising to embrace her destiny as the seaport of the southwest, the new system of boulevards will radiate in every direction, linking with the city the most remote village as well as the thriving centers of various fertile sections of the country. . . .

(1910)

A Delightful Weekend Trip

The near completion of the new boulevard from just below Capistrano through Oceanside and on to San Diego is attracting the attention of Los Angeles motorists to the coast route as a desirable weekend tour. This road follows the ocean so closely that it is one of the coolest trips to be had at this season of the year.

In addition to the coast features of this run as summer trip, there are so many delightful historical associations surrounding the route that it is full of interest to almost every person who is at all familiar with the struggles of the early pioneers and mission fathers who founded the first mission at San Diego and from there gradually fought and prayed their way northerly along what is now the famous "El Camino Real" or "King's Highway."

Not only are there numerous points of interest on the way from Los Angeles to San Diego, but immediately in and around the latter city there are enough attractive runs to induce the travelers to remain several days. Just a brief mention of some of these, without attempting to describe in detail their respective features, may be of interest to motorists contemplating this over Sunday trip along the coast.

First of these popular runs at San Diego may be mentioned Point Loma Drive, eleven miles of as fine a road as can be found anywhere in California. This road, wide, smooth, and a temptation to high speed, encircles the bay and follows the high ridge over swinging curves of easy grade to the old lighthouse built by Uncle Sam on the very tip of Point Loma.

Half way to the point and commanding the highest elevation along the ridge, with a magnificent view up and down the coast and across San Diego Bay, the road passes the arched entrance to the Moorish Temple of Theosophy crowned with a great dome of glass, wherefrom the "Purple Mother" sends forth to her thousands of disciples the teachings of the Order of Theosophical Research.

Another short trip out of San Diego which is popular with motorists is that to Tia Juana, just across the Mexican boundary. It is a sixteen mile drive and usually the roads are good. At Tia Juana the tourist can get a touch of real Mexican life, for here "mañana" is the true spirit of everyone from the smallest urchin to the gaudily dressed matador of the arena, where bull-fighting is the one sport which stirs the Mexican blood to unusual activity.

La Jolla Caves, about twelve miles from San Diego over excellent roads, afford another pleasant run. Here the sandstone cliffs have been deeply serrated by constant attack of Neptune's forces until at certain periods of low tide the resulting caves can be explored to considerable depths. The phantasy of Dante's *Inferno* can well be imagined as centered in La Jolla Caves when the surf booms in and out with ghostly moans and groans of titanic fervor.

While at San Diego a glimpse at least should be taken of the beach and tent city at Coronado, reached by a ten-minute ferry across the Bay.

On the return trip from San Diego one of the first landmarks out of the city is "Twin Palms," set down in old time records as the first palm trees to be grown in California. Their exact age seems to be somewhat indefinite but all agree that they were planted about 1765. They are seen to the right of the road when leaving the city, and are just beyond the old adobe building pointed out as Ramona's home, at which spot, it is said, Ramona was married, and the curious may even get a glimpse of the furnishings of her room.

Near Old Town too, is Mission San Diego, founded in 1769 by Father Junípero Serra. It is in a fair state of preservation and is surely a fitting example of the thoroughness with which the mission padres built all their structures.

Coming up the coast the motor road swings out to Torrey Pines, noted far and wide as the only group of that particular species of pine trees in the United States. The grade from the pines down to Sorrento Cove, a descent of two hundred or more feet, is somewhat steep, but the road bed is wide and no difficulty will be had in negotiating it either up or down.

Del Mar is passed at twenty-four miles from San Diego, and here the tourist will find Stratford Inn, a splendidly appointed modern hostelry. From Del Mar to Oceanside, the new county highway is in the finest possible condition.

About four miles above Oceanside, the old road passes San Luis Rey Mission, founded in 1798. This mission is one of the best preserved of all those forming that famous chain of missions from the Mexican Boundary to San Francisco. . . .

With the completion of the "good roads" work now under construction in San Diego County, it will be but a short time before this two or three day's tour will be the most popular run out of Los Angeles.

(1911)

325 Miles of Roadway

Down in the southwest corner of the United States is San Diego County. Within the limits of San Diego County are mountains and valleys and seacoast, wooded heights and mountain streams and fertile areas. Though large in extent, San Diego County is sparsely settled in comparison with the counties of the Eastern states, but its people have a courage and energy and militant spirit that have accomplished wonders. . . .

Comprised in the three hundred and twenty-five miles of San Diego County's finished roadways are what are known as the Coast Route and Inland Route between San Diego and Los Angeles. The Coast Route extends from San Diego by way of Del Mar, Oceanside and San Onofre to the Orange County line and is one of the most delightful highways that an automobilist can find anywhere. The roadway closely follows the ocean shore, permitting to the traveler a splendid view of the Pacific on one hand and a constantly unfolding panorama of picturesque scenery on the other. The surface of the highway is composed of disintegrated granite and is almost as smooth and hard as a pavement. The Inland Route extends from San Diego through Escondido, Vista, Bonsall and Rainbow to the Riverside County line. This roadway is also finely surfaced and is in splendid condition for touring. . . .

In addition to these completed highways in San Diego there are approximately one hundred miles of fair country roads that may be utilized and, with the rapid progress that is being made, it is only a question of a few months until practically all parts of San Diego County will be open to automobiles. The method of road construction in San Diego County under the Highway Commission has been to surface all roadways, using some good surfacing materials such as disintegrated granite without the use of oil. All who have traveled over these newly constructed roads state that they stand up under use and are superior to roads in other portions of the state that cost much greater amounts to build.

(1912)

What's Good for San Diego . . .
Colonel Ed. Fletcher

Shall San Diego stay on the map of Southern California as a progressive, energetic city, and what advantages have we, if any, in our fight for the Ocean-to-Ocean Highway?

Friendly rivalry among men and towns in the interest of clean sports and for the common good can only bring good results for all. I would consider it a joke for anyone to say that Los Angeles, with its 400,000 people, was jealous of San Diego, a town of 65,000. Los Angeles is the head and controlling factor in Southern California. San Diego is her best customer and does a business of thirty millions with Los Angeles annually.

Anything that helps any city in Southern California helps Los Angeles, and she now and always will get the San Diego travel, both going and coming. Is Los Angeles going to do all she can to divert the Ocean-to-Ocean Highway from San Diego, after knowing the facts? I do not believe it. In the same fraternal spirit of justice and fair play, the writer asks the Ocean-to-Ocean Highway Association, the Automobile Dealers' Association of Los Angeles, the Los Angeles papers, and his friends, to investigate our claims, and if found as represented, to boost our Ocean-to-Ocean Highway in the same spirit that has already made Los Angeles famous, for no good can come to either city that does not help the other.

(1912)

A Large and Joyous "Whoop"

If the Automobile Club of Southern California raises its collective hat and gives voice to one large and joyous "Whoop!" state authorities will have no need to ask the cause of the disturbance.

They will know that it is about the 1915 Motor Tour held by the club in question. . . .

The 1915 "run" was the largest ever held by any motoring organization, in point of the number of automobiles taking part, combined with the long distance— 351 miles—covered. . . . There were no accidents recorded and the two hundred forty-seven cars moving toward San Diego and the Panama-California Exposition arrived, despite threatening weather and April showers, in splendid shape. Moreover, each occupant of those automobiles arrived cheerfully, enthusiastically and in some instances, damply. That perhaps was the greatest triumph of all—the great good spirit of those taking part, their willingness to overlook the minor difficulties, and their eagerness to grasp every opportunity to turn the gloom of the driving rain into the sunshine of happiness.

But the story of the tour is found more definitely in the final analysis of its results.

What did Southern California gain by the 1915 tour? It gained a reputation. There was scarcely a newspaper in America which did not, on the morning of April 24, carry an Associated Press or a United Press account of the excellent condition of Southern California roads which would permit of a continuous tour of one hundred ninety-nine miles by two hundred forty-seven automobiles in a single day. . . .

The day dawned, as days will in and out of books, cloudy, on April 23, with showers in the offing. . . . Led by the Packard "Cactus Kate," and preceded by the "scout car" carrying pennants to those waiting along the route to join the trek, the caravan left Los Angeles on Friday to remain away three days, visiting San Diego and the Exposition. With a single stop, and that for luncheon at Riverside, the cars continued on to their destination through falling rain, over slippery roads with the determination to show the world that it could be done. At no point did the Moon scout car find the sun setting, rising or shining on a discouraged or "peevish" trekker.

In San Diego, the city, the Exposition and the county was theirs. At the county line stood a sign which read: "San Diego County Line—Welcome!" That was the noblest welcome of them all, for the roads had been scraped and rolled, and, it is suspected in some places, swept! Many stopped at the Stratford Inn, Del Mar, for dinner and to look out over the cliffs toward the sea. It was early evening, Del Mar's hour of glory, and looking backward to the valley where "Cactus Kate," like some proud mother, was majestically leading the scores of small black things which were automobiles, it was Southern California's hour of glory, too.

Motor Day, named by the Exposition officials . . . saw the fair teaming with motor cars. They were everywhere, and the sunshine was everywhere and everywhere was good nature.

Instead of returning in a body on Sunday, the motorists followed the vagaries of their own whims and started over the coast road for Los Angeles at any time they saw fit, from daylight until evening. Many stayed over for the Exposition, which no one can possibly see in anything less than a week, if he goes about it thoroughly. If the Automobile Club follows out its intention of holding another tour when the highway is finally completed, it will be assured of at least two hundred forty-seven automobiles which will again take part.

A feature of the tour was the service rendered by the Autocar specially equipped truck, which although declared to be six years old, seemed to be in the prime of life so far as untiring activity was concerned, for it was the mother of the big brood. . . .

(1915)

Scars of the Road

Many aesthetically inclined individuals and organizations have become dismayed at what they term the "despoliation of our landscape" which has resulted from the construction of high-standard arterial highways. Among such organizations is the La Jolla Conservation Society.

In a recent resolution transmitted to public officials it was urged that the counsel of landscape architects be sought when new roads in scenic regions are located and designed.

The viewpoint merits consideration. Highway beautification is a natural succedent to highway construction. Highway improvement still is a relatively new venture in these United States. Highway beautification is even newer. As it has been practiced in the past it has not been an unmixed blessing. Eventually it will be on firm and unerring ground. When it is, proven methods will have been devised that will eliminate much of the original disfigurement, and remedy such as can't be avoided. Even the most offensive of today's scars, we may expect, will disappear with proper treatment or judicious planting of cuts and fills.

(1933)

III
A Dictionary of
San Diego Land Names

Phil Townsend Hanna

———◆─◆◆◆─◆———

In the 1930s, the late Phil Townsend Hanna, then editor of *Westways*, embarked on a series entitled, "California Names—A Gazetteer." Each month thirty or forty new California place names would be listed and their genealogies and histories traced, whether Indian, Spanish or real estate subdivision. "Names," Hanna later wrote, "are stories— sad stories, glad stories, amazing stories, amusing stories." What follows are fifty-six such "stories" from San Diego County.

AGUA CALIENTE SPRINGS. *(Sp.—Ah'-gwah Kah-lee-ehn'-teh).* A name common in California, in this instance the origin being unrevealed. The words are Spanish, meaning "hot water".

ALPINE. A small settlement started about 1883 by Benjamin R. Arnold, a New England importer of ivory, who came to California seeking relief from asthma. Finding the locality a healthful one, he established a town, grocery store, town hall, and small library.

BARRETT. Named for George and William Barrett who resided here in the seventies. Barrett Dam and Lake, an artificial water reservoir draining 130 square miles, take their name from them.

BONITA. *(Sp.—Boh-neé-tah).* A community established in the Sweetwater Valley and designated with the Spanish word meaning "pretty".

BOSTONIA. A settlement of 1887 made by a group of Boston colonists who bought a tract of 500 acres and started the cultivation of citrus fruits and raisin grapes. It was likewise known as the "Boston Ranch".

BUCKMAN SPRINGS. Long known to the Indians, the springs named for Col. Amos Buckman, pioneer prospector of the 'sixties whose name they bear, were held sacred by the aborigines. One of their legends relates that the lovely Fanita, daughter of Chief Cuyamaca, nursed her lover Carissa, back to health with the lithia water for which the springs are noted. The springs were developed and the water marketed in 1870.

CABRILLO NATIONAL MONUMENT. *(Kah-breel'-yoh).* This monument, half an acre in size, was created by presidential proclamation on October 14, 1913, to preserve the first landing place of Juan Rodriguez Cabrillo in California in 1542. (See *San Diego*).

CAMPO. *(Sp.—Kahm'-poh).* Being an Indian settlement, Campo's name (Sp.—"camp") was a natural for the first Spanish visitors. First Americans to settle here in 1870 were emigrants from Texas, hence the community was known colloquially as Little Texas, or New Texas.

CARLSBAD. When in 1887 springs were discovered here bearing practically the same mineral content as the waters of Karlsbad, Bohemia (Germ.—Charles' Watering-place, for Emperor Charles IV, circa 1347) the locality fell heir to the name of the famous German spa. In a burst of patriotic fervor during the First World War, the name was clipped to "Carl", but when the war hysteria subsided the original name was restored.

CARRIZO. *(Sp.—Kah-ree'-zoh).* Carrizo (Sp.—"reedgrass") exudes a sap containing a sweet substance. The Indians made a form of sugar from the sap which they traded with the Mexicans. Much of the grass once grew in this locality, a popular water-hole of the arid places, and once a station on the Butterfield Overland Stage line.

CHULA VISTA. *(Sp.—Choo'-lah Vee'-stah).* Part of the original Rancho Nacional of 26,631 acres, operated by the presidio of San Diego in 1828 and confirmed to Juan Forster in 1858, Chula Vista was one of a number of communities established during the boom period of 1887. There was much competition for alluring names among the town-site promoters of the period and it is hardly strange that they chose this cognomen, meaning "pretty view".

CLEVELAND NATIONAL FOREST. Created as

a merger of Trabuco Canyon and San Jacinto National forests by an executive order of President Theodore Roosevelt, on July 1, 1908. It was named for President Grover Cleveland, who died on June 24, about a week previous to the signing of the order.

CORONADO. *(Sp.—Koh-roh-nah'-doh).* Not for Francisco Vásquez de Coronado, intrepid Spanish explorer and conqueror who entered the Far Southwest in 1540, but for Los Cuatro Martires Coronados (the Four Crowned Martyrs) was Coronado named. The peninsula that encloses San Diego Bay attained its name indirectly from the offshore Coronado Islands (Las Islas Coronados). Juan Rodríguez Cabrillo first sighted the islands on September 17, 1542. He called them Islas Desiertas (Deserted Islands). When Sebastian Vizcaino reached them on November 8, 1602, he called them San Martin. But Father Antonio de la Ascension named them Los Cuatros Martires Coronados, in view of the fact that they were four in number and that they were sighted on the saint's day of the four martyrs. Incidentally the Four Crowned Martyrs were four christians —Severus, Severianus, Carpophorus and Victorinus, scourged to death in Rome under Diocletian, in 303 A.D. . . . It was acquired by Archibald C. Peachy and William H. Aspinwall from Pedro C. Carrillo for $110,-000 on June 11, 1869, and in 1885 passed to a syndicate which in 1886 took the name of the islands and became known as the Coronado Beach Co. The renowned hotel was built in 1888, with John D. Spreckels as sole owner. The area at one time was also known as the Peachy and Aspinwall Peninsula.

CORTE MADERA MOUNTAIN. *(Sp.—Kohr'-teh Mah-deh'-rah).* Origin unrevealed. The words are Spanish, meaning "wood cutting place".

CUYAMACA. *(Ind.—Kwee-yah-mah'-kah).* Cuyamaca originally was an Indian *ranchería* and a *visita* of San Diego Mission, also known as "Cuyamai", "Guia-mac", and "Cuyamac". The legends of the Diegueños tell of a Chief Cuyamaca, though whether the chief took his name from, or gave his name to, the *ranchería,* is unrevealed. The name, according to T. T. Waterman, University of California anthropologist, derives from the two Indian words "Kwe", meaning "rain", and "Amak", meaning "yonder". He thinks that it was first applied to Cuyamaca Mountain, which with Cuyamaca Lake (known likewise in the early days as La Laguna Que se Seca; Sp.—"The Lake That Dries Up") stems from the root name.

DEHESA. *(Sp.—Deh-heh'-sah).* Origin of name unrevealed. The word is Spanish meaning "pasturage".

DEL MAR. *(Sp.—Dehl Mahr')* Meaning "of the sea", or "by the sea", Del Mar was originally projected by T. M. Hoop as a literary and art center, perhaps as early as 1886. It, too, was one of San Diego County's boom towns.

DESCANO. *(Sp.—Deh-skahn'-soh).* Sereval thoroughly plausible explanations of the origin of the name Descanso (Sp.—"place of rest") are advanced. Local historians insist that it gained its name from the fact that a party of surveyors running the lines of the old ranch grants, stopped here each day for their lunch.

DULZURA. *(Dool-zoo'-rah).* A Spanish word meaning "sweetness", Dulzura is said to have attained its name because it was a center for milk and honey production.

EL CAJON. *(Sp.—El Kah-hohn').* El Cajon derives its name from the Rancho El Cajon which, in turn, was named for the valley in which the ranch was located, the valley originating in a *cajon* (Sp.—"box") canyon hemmed in by lofty and precipitous mountains. Near the present town of El Cajon, the fathers of San Diego Mission tilled a vineyard for many years.

ENCANTO. *(Sp.—En-kahn'-toh).* A salubrious climate, coupled with "enchanting" views of San Diego and the Pacific, caused the bestowal of this euphonious Spanish name on a station on the San Diego and Eastern Railroad, by Miss Ella Klauber, in 1889 or 1890. In about 1891 a part of the original tract was subdivided and this name was given to the subdivision.

ENCINITAS. *(Sp.—Ehn-see-nee'-tahs).* The name is Spanish, meaning "little evergreen oaks", and presumably the locality was named after the Spanish grant upon which it was situated—Encinitos Rancho. The townsite was laid out in 1883.

ESCONDIDO. *(Sp.—Eh-skohn-dee'-doh).* Meaning "hidden", this community was so named very probably in virtue of its location on the floor of an inland valley. . . . It was purchased in 1885 by San Diego and Los Angeles capitalists who subdivided it into small farms and town lots.

FLINN SPRINGS. A pioneer of 1864, William E. Flinn, sheep and cattleman, gave his name to these springs of pure water—a popular stopping place on the long and arid journey of freighters and stages between Yuma and San Diego.

GASKILL PEAK. Named for an early settler, whose full cognomen has been lost in antiquity. Ruins of Gaskill's old adobe home still stand on the mountain homesite where he lived.

GUATAY. *(Ind.—Wah'-tye).* A Diegueño Indian word, meaning "large" which is said originally to have been applied to Guatay Mountain because the Indians thought it resembled a large wigwam.

HIPASS. A corruption of "high pass" and so named because it is the highest point on the San Diego and Arizona Railroad, with an elevation of 3660 ft.

HULBURD GROVE. A popular year-'round resort and mountain homesite tract named for Ebenezer Wallace Hulburd, of Kansas City, who, with Dr. Frederick D. C. Meyers and Justin Robinson, settled there in 1884 to regain failing health and to pursue the metaphysical mysteries of spiritualism, to which the trio were devoted. Later the ranch was given over to cattle. The Meyers' cabin, scene of many an old-time seance, still stands, but the resort is chiefly noted for its numerous huge live oaks.

JACUMBA. *(Ind.—Hah-Koom'-bah).* A Diegueño Indian word said to mean "hut-by-the-water" and probably occasioned by the presence here beside Jacumba's noted hot-and-cold artesian springs of an Indian dwelling.

JAMACHA. *(Ind.—Hah-mah-chah').* A Diegueño Indian *rancheria,* variously spelled "Jamacha", "Jamacho" and "Hamacha", and known by the mission fathers as "San Jacomé de la Marca". The Indian word means "wild squash plant". It is believed that the rebellious Indians who destroyed San Diego Mission on November 4, 1775, and massacred Father Luís Jayme came from Jamacha. A local legend locates the elusive Pegleg mine three miles east of the settlement.

JAMUL. *(Ind.—Hah-mool').* A Diegueño *rancheria* and *visita* of San Diego Mission. The word means "foam" or "lather". The region was employed by the mission fathers as winter pasturage for their livestock. Rancho Jamul was granted to Pío Pico in 1831, but the U. S. Land Commission later declined to confirm Pico's title.

LAGUNA LAKES. *(Sp.—Lah-goo'nah.)* The name is an unnecessarily repetitive one for "laguna" in Spanish means "lake". "Las Lagunas" or "Lagunas" would have been better usage. "Lakes" is an irritating appendage. The origin of the name is unrevealed but it designates one of the largest public recreational areas established by the U. S. Forest Service in California, located in the Cleveland National Forest.

LA JOLLA. Much mystery surrounds the name of La Jolla for it is neither Spanish nor Indian. What it sounds like is a poor American attempt to Hispanicize, onomatopoetically, a perfectly good Spanish phrase, notably "La Joya", or "the jewel", as a result of the caves located there. The town-site of La Jolla was established by F. T. Botsford in 1887, though whether he is responsible for this corruption is not revealed.

LAKE HODGES. Located on the San Dieguito River and known as the Carroll reservoir site, it was part of the property in and about Warner's Ranch acquired in 1911 by William Griffith Hinshaw, moving spirit in the development of San Diego County's back-country water supply. The Hodges Dam, named for W. E. Hodges, vice-president of the Santa Fe Railway, was financed by the Santa Fe Land Improvement Co., a subsidiary, in 1917. The dam formed a lake with a capacity of 37,000 acre feet.

LA MESA. Origin of name is unrevealed. The word is Spanish, meaning "table" and is frequently applied to flat table-like areas of land. The name is not especially aptly applied in this instance.

LINDA VISTA. *(Sp.—Leen'-dah Veé-stah).* The name is Spanish, meaning "beautiful view" but its origin is unrevealed.

MIRAMAR. *(Sp.—Meé-rah-mahr).* Meaning "sea view", Miramar was first applied to his Linda Vista Ranch by E. W. Scripps. The post office of Miramar was established in April, 1892. The name is a popular one in Spanish-speaking lands for country homes. It was the name given to the Spanish royal chalet located at San Sebastian, on the Bay of Biscay.

MORENA LAKE. *(Sp.—Moh-reh'-nah).* An artificial reservoir of 17,493,000,000 gal. capacity and a vital part of San Diego City's water system. The origin of the name is unrevealed; the word is Spanish, meaning "brown". In 1915 C. M. Hatfield, the "rainmaker", used the lake as a site for his precipitation experiments. Water reserves being low, the San Diego City Council entered a contract with him. Hatfield proceeded with his operation, and disastrous floods supervened, washing out lower Otay Dam, and filling Morena Lake to within 18 inches of capacity. Hatfield threatened to sue for his fee and the city retaliated with threats of a suit for the damage that resulted. Controversy was settled out of court.

NATIONAL CITY. Situated on the Rancho Nacional, Rancho del Rey or Rancho la Purísima, as it was variously known, granted some time between 1820 and 1830, and operated by the presidio of San Diego in 1828, National City took its Americanized name shortly after 1868 when a portion of the ranch was purchased by the Kimball brothers and a townsite was established.

NESTOR. Nestor was established in 1893 and named for one of its early settlers, M. C. Nestor Young.

OTAY. *(Ind.—Oh'-tay).* Otay, a Diegueño Indian name meaning "brushy", was first applied to one of the numerous aboriginal *rancherías* in the San Diego back country. The Otay Rancho, named after the *ranchería,* was first granted to José A. Estudillo in 1829. Otay Lake and Otay Mountain stem from the original name.

PACIFIC BEACH. Intended as an educational center, Pacific Beach (the name is obvious and commonplace) was founded in 1887—the bigger and better boom year. It was the site of the San Diego College of Letters, of which Samuel Sprecher was president and Harr Wagner, vice-president. The college was abandoned when the promotional sky-rocket fell with a thud in the 1890's.

PALA. A village on the Pala Indian Reservation

inhabited by Luiseño Indians who were evicted from their rancherías in the vicinity of Warner's Ranch in May, 1903. The word is Luiseño, meaning "water" or "place of water". The ranchería was first noted by Father Juan Mariner who explored the region in 1795. It is first named by Father Antonio Peyri, in his annual report dated December 31, 1810, wherein he records that a granary had been built at "Rancho de Pala". In 1816, Father Peyri built the chapel of San Antonio de Pala, as an *asistencia* of San Luís Rey Mission. It still stands as one of the best preserved structures of mission days, particularly distinguished for its detached campanile.

POINT LOMA. *(Sp.—Loh'-mah).* Point Loma, or "Hill Point" first appeared on a map of San Diego and vicinity drawn by Juan Pantoja in 1782. It was there designated as "Punta de la Loma", quite naturally as a result of its precipitous elevation above the sea. A small outpost of old San Diego known as La Playa was located here at one time, and the so-called "Old Spanish Light-house", which was not Spanish in origin but rather American, was established after the point was made a military reservation in 1852.

PONTO. *(Sp.—Pohn'-toh).* The origin of the name is unrevealed, but it's poetical Spanish for "the sea". The point was first known as "La Costa", as early as 1893, and was changed to its present form in June, 1918.

POTRERO. *(Sp.—Poh-treh'-roh).* Origin of name is unrevealed. It is a Spanish word, meaning "pasture".

POWAY. *(Ind.—Poh'-way).* Very probably an English corruption of "Pawaii", a Diegueño and Luiseño Indian word meaning "meeting of the valleys."

RANCH HOUSE. A station on the original Southern California Railway named as early as 1897 because it served the home ranch-house of the Santa Margarita y las Flores Rancho.

RANCHO SANTA FE. *(Sp.—Rahn'-choh Sahn'-tah Feh).* Developed in 1922, with the completion of the Lake Hodges irrigation system, as high-class country estates, by the Santa Fe Land Improvement Co., a subsidiary of the Santa Fe Railway. Originally the ranch, a part of the San Dieguito Rancho, was employed by the railway to grow eucalypti for ties, but the wood proved unsuitable.

SAN DIEGO. *(Sp.—Sahn Dee-yah'-goh).* First white to see San Diego Bay, from which the city, county and mission take their names, was Juan Rodriguez Cabrillo, who visited it on Sept. 29, 1542, calling it San Miguel (St. Michael the Archangel) whose feast day it was. Sebastian Vizcaino reached the bay on November 10, 1602, and remained several days. On the 12th the expedition, accompanied by Carmelite friar companions went ashore to attend mass. It being the saint's day of San Diego de Alcalá, Vizcaino gave it this name. Common tendency has been to render San Diego as "St. James", but ecclesiastics insist the name is that of St. Didacus, a Franciscan lay-brother who aided missionaries of the order in the Canary Islands in the Fifteenth Century and died in the convent of Alcalá in Castile, in 1463. He was canonized in virtue of the many miracles worked at his tomb. When the Sacred Expedition, headed by Father Junípero Serra and Don Gaspar de Portolá, reached San Diego Bay on July 16, 1769, first settlement was established at the Indian *ranchería* of Cosoy, where Old Town now is located.

SAN DIEGO MISSION. The mission of San Diego de Alcalá (St. Didacus of Alcalá), first of the chain of California missions, was originally established on July 16, 1769, at the Indian *ranchería* of Cosoy, now known as Old Town, on San Diego Bay, by Father Junípero

Serra. In August, 1774, the mission was moved to another Indian *ranchería* called Nipaguay, its present site in Mission Valley, in virtue of the lack of water at Cosoy, and the exposure of the neophytes there to defilement by the soldiers.

SAN ISIDRO. *(Sp.—Sahn Ee-seé-droh).* A *sitio*, meaning, in Spanish, "country seat" or "villa", established by the presidio of San Diego some time between 1820 and 1830 and named for St. Isidore of Seville, Bishop of Seville, A.D. 600. It is now the closest American community to the Mexican border on U. S. Highway No. 101 [Interstate 5].

SAN LUIS REY MISSION. *(Sp.—Sahn Loo-ees' Reh).* Eighteenth Franciscan mission in Alta California, San Luís Rey was founded by Fathers Fermín Francisco Lasuén, Antonio Peyri and Juan José Norberto Santiago on June 13, 1798. It was formally named San Luís Rey de Francia, after St. Louis IX (April 25, 1215-August 25, 1270) King of France. Father Juan Crespí, accompanying the Portolá expedition of 1769, camped on the spot on July 18 and remarked: "I gave this valley the name of San Juan Capistrano, for a mission." The mission of this name subsequently, however, was located at an entirely different place. The San Luís Rey River takes its name from the mission.

SAN MARCOS. *(Sp.—Sahn Mahr'-kohs).* San Marcos takes its name from the valley, a grant to San Luís Rey Mission known as Los Vallecitos de San Marcos—"the little valleys of St. Mark"—the latter being the author of one of the four Gospels.

SANTA MARGARITA Y LAS FLORES RANCHO. *(Sp.—Sahn'-tah Mahr-gah-ree'-tah ee Lahs Floh'-rehs).* One of the truly great ranches of California, granted in 1841 to Pío and Andrés Pico, and which later became the object of extended litigation between the Picos and their brother-in-law, Don Juan

Forster. The ranch takes its name from two camps established upon it by Don Gaspar de Portolá and Father Juan Crespí during the course of their expedition of 1769 in search of Monterey. On July 20, the party rested at a spot which Crespí called Santa Margarita (for St. Margaret, a Third Century martyr of Antioch, whose saint's day it was).

SORRENTO. Located within the present city limits of San Diego, Sorrento was sub-divided in 1887. It took its name from Italy's famous Sorrento.

TECATE. *(Ind.—Teh-kah'-teh).* Originally an Indian *ranchería* and *visíta* of San Diego Mission, it was granted as Rancho Tecate to Juan Bandini, who operated it in 1836. The community was established in the 'eighties with the opening of a store by one Greer. It is now a border port of entry between Mexico and the United States.

VALLECITO. *(Sp.—Vahl-yeh-see'-toh).* Origin of name is unrevealed. The word is Spanish meaning "little valley". It was referred to as "Bayo Cita" and "Bayeau Chitoes" by soldiers in General Stephen W. Kearny's Army of the West, which reached this camping place on November 29, 1846. During the life of the Butterfield Overland Stage Line (August 31, 1757-August 2, 1861) Vallecito was an important stage station. Lately the old adobe station has been restored by historically-minded San Diego County residents, and the area about it is proposed as an addition to the Anza State Park.

IV
Along the Shore

Any summer Sunday's drive along the coast highway will quickly prove the tremendous drawing power of San Diego County's fine beaches. The influx of seaside pleasure seekers really began back in the 1880s, the period of Southern California's first great real estate and resort boom. Two of San Diego's truly opulent watering places were the Hotel Del Coronado and the Casa del Mar. And though the Casa del Mar began to fail almost from the moment it was completed, the Coronado thrives today as it has for nearly ninety years.

Unsigned articles in this chapter are "Coronado's Silver Strand" and "Ahoy! La Jolla." Both appeared in the 1920s during the editorship of William M. Henry, later to be known as Bill Henry, popular columnist for the Los Angeles *Times*. Both articles are fine, though regrettably anonymous, examples of some of the most empurpled descriptive writing ever to appear in *Touring Topics* or *Westways*.

Coronado's Silver Strand

The instant impression of Coronado Beach is beauty. Not in one, but in all things. Sea, sky and surroundings combine in one harmonious effect to stamp idelibly on the memory the recollection of a haunting and unusual picture of unique loveliness. And perhaps most vividly to the looker-on is brought the sense of a deep serenity, a lull in the hurrying order of things mundane, as though the sea itself had sought a sheltering harbor, and now, steeped in a delicious calm, was rocked in a happy dream of *dolce far niente*. Over the bright blue waters the gulls soar and dip, and over the gulls the distant dome of placid skies rims down to the distant horizon. What matters the bustle and stir of the outside world, the whir of machinery, or the long line of smoke that marks the course of an outbound freighter? Here there is only the subduing influence of nature, the visions and echoes of cloistered charm to meet and greet the partaker of these delights.

A brilliantly-tinted red parasol swung idly from the hand of a passing girl flashes suddenly a vignette of color against the gray sands. Down on the beach, gaudy and sombre-hued umbrellas are planted, and under them lounge the "sand-lizards" or "beach hounds," wallowing in the warm sand, basking and sleeping in the sun-waves that beat about their canvas retreats, and occasionally rising and taking a dip in the waters that curl and rustle along the edges of the tawny sands. . . .

Doubtless few beaches the world over enjoy the advantages of a more varied or more alluring programme of enjoyment than Coronado. The main coast yachting events are held there, and the crucial tennis tournaments of the year are played at Coronado. Many of the most famous swimming records have been made in its waters, while the polo grounds, and the fierce contests of this notably virile sport at these grounds, have caused the name and reputation of Coronado to be known as well as the English and Continental centers of the "pony-to-pony" game. It is this infinite variety of attraction, coupled with the superb beach and surf bathing facilities, which puts Coronado on such a high plane among seacoast resorts the world over.

A special magnet of interest is the Naval Air Station, within a mile of the Hotel Del Coronado, where the very center of aerial experiment and development in the United States is located. Every day the air is dotted with airplanes going through their maneuvers and glidings, and excepting to the occasional visitor, the sight of an airship, or a flock of "sky-scrapers" is very much a matter of course. But to the student of events, to the man who is keeping in touch with the trend of the times, there can be no fascinating problem to attack while he is making a visit to Coronado. Both in peace and in war, the future of the airplane is one of the greatest possibilities of modern invention, and the Naval Air Station is in reality a University of National Defense. . . .

(1922)

The Coronado Carries On

Curtis Zahn

The hotel was, and is, the hub. A polo grounds, ostrich farm, boat club, railroad and ferryboat all became actual facts once construction started. Stores and dwellings, shops and farms served no other purpose than contributing to the mechanical function of the gargantua. Guests came from every country to enjoy the astonishing climate, and prominent authors were moved to write strange, not unflowery, odes after a stay by the bay.

Edison came to marvel at the first and largest installation of the new incandescent lamp—ten thousand of them—supplied by a wheezing power plant which later supplied the growing village and still furnishes the only electricity used by the hotel.

The case history bulges with the purple lavishness of the desperate 'nineties; hundred-dollar bills were found under dinner plates—to be used for gambling in the madcap Silver Grill which was (reportedly) built on tidelands so that city ordinances couldn't interfere.

Today—despite three wars, seven depressions and visits by four presidents—the hotel is almost the same as ever.

(1946)

Ahoy! La Jolla

The little, Spanish-named seaside city lay like a jewel in the sunlight, ringed in by a shining circlet of the bluest of azure seas. Surely there never was a more fascinating ocean crescent than that which holds La Jolla in its clasp of glittering sands and tidal murmurs. As we drove our automobile along the highway and looked out over the Pacific, a wall of foam-crested waters broke heavily against broad battlements of rugged stone, and the flash of white spray followed as the baffled tides fell back in a welter of tossing and wrinkled brine.

Groups and clusters of surf bathers were entering the breakers or standing at the water's edge as we went down to the beach. Some of the more expert swimmers were already beyond the first line of rollers, and others, less adventurous, were paddling and splashing in the shallower water close inshore. Brown-bodied and bare-limbed "kiddies" were much in evidence, their clear eyes and springy movements attesting to the vitality born of sunlight, sea water, and fresh breezes.

A Dip in the Surf

We were soon in the surf ourselves, and who that has dipped into the sparkling sea currents of the La Jolla beaches will ever forget the thrill and uplift of such an experience? The water was as exhilarating as wine, just cool enough to be bracing, but without any undue chill, and the tides were coming in with a sufficient sweep to make "riding the breakers" the very acme of maritime sport. It was like being caught in a liquid, giantlike grasp, and then being carried shoreward in mid air.

For more than an hour we swam, floated, and rode the curving rollers before returning to the sands to laze about in the warm surface, and enjoy a soaking sunbath. . . .

As the afternoon wore on the beaches and rocks were thronged with swimmers and loungers, and the crowds moved up and down the shore enjoying the varied sights and spectacles. . . .

A Gorgeous Sunset

Another plunge in the inviting salt water just before sundown gave us a new sensation of delight and we stayed in until the western gates were ablaze with the tints and varying colors of the descending sun. La Jolla itself lay in comparative shadow. Its trees and shrubbery, its vines and flowers were already enveloped in the folds of the gathering twilight. But westward to the distant horizon the sea was aflame with coruscating rays of scarlet and crimson, that made the sky a wavering picture of indescribable brilliance. One lone star stood out beyond The Crocodile's Head, and at the cave entrances a dusky curtain now hung that swathed their arches in a shroud of deepest gloom.

The swimmers were gradually deserting the beaches and the breakers, and before we had dressed there were scarcely a dozen loiterers left. More stars had hung out their lanterns, and the sickle of a new moon shone ivory-pale to the far northeast. . . .

And so we said goodbye to La Jolla, the unique and the beautiful, resting calmly in its semicircle of brooding sands and hushed waters, lovely alike by either night or day, superb in its surroundings of color, life and motion; a true sea opal, paling and glowing under sunshine or moonlight, and now wrapped in a mantle of sombre shadows and brightly-glittering stars.

(1922)

The Rise and Fall of Old Del Mar

Kenneth C. Reiley

At Torrey Pines beach, six miles west of his 7,000-acre Rancho Las Penasquitas, Colonel Jacob Shell Taylor swung the chestnut stallion up the dusty road that led to a barren mesa.

Thirty minutes later, on this sunny day in 1882, Taylor had purchased 160 acres on the site of the present Del Mar. Six months later streets were laid out.

Taylor, former Indian scout for Buffalo Bill Cody, surveyor and one of the wealthiest men in San Diego County, was about to fulfill his dream of a swank beach town, with an elaborate hotel and resultant subdivision of the lands surrounding it.

And he succeeded in making Del Mar the showplace of the south coast, the gathering place for the political and social elite of booming Southern California.

Newspaper accounts of Old Del Mar's rise and fall are plentiful, and all mention the intrepid colonel of the Grand Army of the Republic, his wit, his good looks and his skill with his fists and six-gun.

By 1884 what is now a quiet resort community was a bustling town of 200. Dust churned from its 100-foot wide streets as wagonload after wagonload of lumber went into new homes and shops. . . .

In 1885, Taylor broke ground for Casa del Mar, an eighty-room hotel that rivaled San Diego's storied Horton House.

He spent $15,000 for 50,000 board feet of cedar, redwood and pine, and ordered his architect to pattern the Casa after the swank Florence Hotel in San Diego.

The result was an elaborate hostelry, 140 feet wide, two stories high and surrounded by a spacious veranda. Flags flew from it by day and oil street lights illuminated it by night.

Its ballroom became the setting for musicals, recitals and weekend dances attended by the socially elite from San Diego, a scant hour distant by California Southern Railroad, forerunner of the Santa Fe.

It served as hospital, town hall and clearing house for community problems. It housed a Grand Army of the Republic convention and played host to Governor R. W. Waterman who was so moved by its elegance that he delivered a thirty-minute speech from the veranda following an ostrich omelet breakfast. . . .

Meanwhile Taylor was busy attracting more and more persons to his hotel. The weekly dances, the social events and hunting excursions at times gave way to more theatrical publicity attempts.

Traveling shows pitched tents near the hotel and were hissed and booed out of town. He conducted carriage races on the beach, and saw one participant almost drown.

Then in 1887 the California land boom began to fizzle and his lots went a-begging. Business at the hotel dwindled to a few steady customers and the cabanas stood empty for long periods.

For two years Taylor fought the changing times, but in 1889, three years after he opened the hotel, disaster literally rained down on Del Mar.

Great rains washed out bridges and roads. The colonel's private telephone line to San Diego was cut, and the California Southern Railroad stopped running.

Del Mar was marooned, its paths to the beach impassible, its gardens washed away, and its hogs and chickens drowned.

The gay spirit of the hotel was broken. A number of the remaining guests departed as soon as transportation became available.

Then, on January 17, 1890, the end came to Casa del Mar. A fire broke out in the kitchen at 2 A.M. and in two hours the proud hotel was reduced to ashes. . . .

The South Coast Land Company in 1915 built the present Hotel Del Mar, a half mile to the north. There they relocated the town, after destroying the last vestiges of Casa del Mar. The pavilions were razed, the beach pool was dynamited and the four-story lookout tower, from which the townsfolk once could view Catalina, was leveled.

Only the little pergola at the top of the cliff and the crumbling cement pilings of the beach swimming pool remain to mark the site of the luxurious Casa del Mar. Its life was short but gay.

(1959)

The *Silver Gate* Saga
Jerry MacMullen

"A select group of about twenty-five ladies and gentlemen braved the rainy weather yesterday to make a short voyage on the Coronado Beach Company's new ferry boat, *Silver Gate*. Only one boiler was used and the speed, therefore, was slow, but the action of the machinery showed that the vessel is perfect in that department."

That brief item in the *San Diego Union* for March 5, 1888, heralded the commissioning of a vessel which was to become, in the order named, the beach company's pride and joy, a community joke, and a landmark of the San Diego and Coronado waterfronts. Years ahead of her time, she was the first ferry vessel in California—if not in the country—which had propellers instead of the traditional sidewheels. She was the largest steamer ever built on San Diego Bay for peacetime use, and it was not until forty-three years later that she was equaled in size by any ferry vessel in Southern California.

Back in those days of gas jets and Congress gaiters, Coronado was not lacking in industrial enterprises. There was a shipyard—where the 528-ton ferry and numerous steam tugs and launches were built—and there was a foundry, whose products in 1888 included a huge nine-foot, cast-iron "winder" for the powerhouse of the old Temple Street Cable Railway in Los Angeles. Down the Silver Strand to the south of Coronado was a brickyard which made the bricks for the foundations and chimneys of Hotel del Coronado, its site still being known to yachtsmen and picnickers as Brickyard Cove. All traces of these establishments have vanished these many years ago.

The *Silver Gate* was nothing if not a novelty, in architecture as well as machinery. In general appearance, she somewhat resembled a wedding-cake, what with the jig-saw work which dripped like wooden icicles from the edge of her hurricane deck, and the scrolls and turnings and gimcracks which adorned her glass-enclosed passenger cabin. The lower deck was paved with asphalt, which was more than one could say for Coronado's streets at the time, and was designed to accommodate "at least fifty teams without crowding." Topping off this delightful bit of maritime Victoriana were two pilot-houses whose roofs seem to have been a grand success, but to the vessel's owners it was a bit disappointing; it had taken their fine new steamboat twelve minutes to cross the bay, which is less than half a mile wide. This is not quite three miles an hour, any way you look at it. So they tinkered around, put on different propellers and eventually whittled it down to six minutes, which still was none too good. Finally, on April 6, she was placed in service.

Propeller design was, in those days, a bit on the haphazard side. They soon learned that it took a long time to get the *Silver Gate* started. Just as quickly, but more expensively, they found that it took a long time to get her stopped, and while they were stopping her she had her own ideas about where she was going. On the second night of her service, she missed the ferry slip completely, bashed in a nearby wharf and conducted herself in a generally undignified manner before Captain A. P. Bunker finally got her into the slip, an hour and a half later. A squib in the morning paper of April 10 announced that Captain Bunker wasn't with the ferry company any more, but did not indicate whether he merely left in high dudgeon or departed under the then popular belief that any corporation could solve any problem merely by sacking someone. Anyhow, it didn't cure the *Silver Gate* of her hoydenish tricks, and on April 17 she was laid up for some more hopeful tinkering. A fortnight later she was at it again, and on May 6 we find the following choice waterfront tid-bit in the *Union*:

"The ferry steamer *Silver Gate,* which has nearly ruined the slips on both sides of the bay, will be returned to the Union Iron Works at San Francisco. The Coronado Beach Company claims that the Union Iron Works did not fulfill their contract, and it is probable that a suit for damages will also be commenced by the Beach people."

Just how one goes about "returning" a steamboat to an iron works where it never has been is something which the story left out. . . .

They tied up the *Silver Gate* at the ferry wharf in Coronado, and there she lay from 1888 until 1902. In drawingroom and grog shop her name became a byword, and as time passed, her infamy grew. She was top-heavy. She wouldn't steer. She was haunted. She used to frighten little children—in short, she was a very bad girl indeed. In 1902 they took out her engines and sold them to some mine in Mexico. Big glass windows were installed all around her, a hardwood floor was laid on her lower deck, and they towed her up into Glorietta Bay where, under the name *Casino,* she became a floating dance hall and club room for Coronado Tent City, that now vanished summer resort of fond memory. In 1910 a big dance pavilion was built ashore, and the *Casino,* neé *Silver Gate,* was sold to the San Diego Yacht Club, which towed her over to the foot of Hawthorne Street, on the San Diego side of the bay.

The yachtsmen had a lot of fun with her in the four years which followed. The fun included a big regatta for which funds were needed. . . . So they stripped off her copper sheathing and sold it for junk. And from then on her pine planking, thus exposed by the removal of the copper, was enjoyed by teeming thousands of teredoes and other forms of marine life having sharp teeth and destructive habits. That, of course, made her leak like a sieve, and it took a sizeable bilge pump to keep her afloat.

In 1914, harbor improvements forced her removal to a new location. So, one Sunday morning, the larger power yachts took her in tow and hauled her back to Coronado, not far from the place where, once before, she had lain for a dozen years. There was no more talk of even trying to keep her afloat any more; they just beached her, sideways, at the peak of the flood tide, and built a connecting wharf to the shore. From then on, the tide merely rose and fell inside her ageing hull. Around 1920 the dry rot in her upperworks got to the point where it no longer could be ignored; she was sold to a firm of housewreckers, and was broken up.

Along the north shore of Coronado, in front of the Waves' barracks, you can see, at low tide, a row of jumbled cobblestones. There are few around Coronado today who recognize those rocks as the ballast which kept the *Silver Gate* right side up.

(1945)

V
San Diego Superlatives

In late 1935, a "California Superlatives" contest was held by *Westways* magazine.

"Do you know the longest river, the tallest building, the oldest living native in California?" the invitation read. "*Westways* will pay $2.50 for each such superlative reported, with reference to competent authority. . . ."

All of the winning San Diego superlatives are here reprinted, along with one lone diminutive, which somehow slipped by "competent authority."

Oldest planted tree in California is the Serra Palm by Presidio Hill, Old Town, San Diego. It was planted by Fr. Junípero Serra in July, 1769, and marks the site of the first permanent Spanish camp and the burial place of many of those who came to California with the first expedition.

Oldest living olive trees in California are those at Misión San Diego de Alcalá, the cuttings of which were brought from Mexico City in 1794.

Oldest living pepper tree in California is in the garden at Misión San Luis Rey, San Diego County. It was planted by Padre Antonio Peyri in 1830 and grew from some seeds given to him by a sailor from Peru.

Jane Elizabeth Adams, San Diego

Farthest southwest post office in California (and in the United States) is at Nestor, in San Diego County.

Tom Cummins, Ontario

Biggest bird cage in California is in Balboa Park, San Diego. It is 100 feet high and has just been completed to house the larger birds.

Harlan L. Wilson, San Diego

97

Oldest mission in California is Misión San Diego de Alcalá, founded on July 16, 1769, by Father Junípero Serra.

Viola E. Hoffman, Manhattan Beach

Largest outdoor pipe organ in California is in Balboa Park, San Diego.

Bertha A. Singer, San Diego

Smallest national monument in California is the Cabrillo National Monument which marks the landing of Juan Rodríguez Cabrillo in 1542 on what is now Point Loma in San Diego County. It covers one-half of one acre.

Douglas S. Adams, Los Angeles

Earliest printing in California was a woodblock letterhead. The actual date of its printing is unknown, but a letter written on it, signed by Governor José María Echeandía and dated at San Diego, October 30, 1826, is preserved in the office of the Recorder of Santa Cruz County, Santa Cruz.

Glen Dawson, Los Angeles

Largest telescope in California is in the Mt. Wilson Observatory. It has a 100-inch reflector. The new 200-inch reflector now under construction will be housed in an observatory on Palomar Mountain in San Diego County.

Tom G. Bastyr, Monrovia

Largest early California rancho remaining intact today is the Rancho Santa Margarita y las Flores in northern San Diego and southern Orange counties. When owned by Andrés and Pío Pico it contained some 89,000 acres, but now numbers over 200,000 acres. It is soon to be subdivided.

Bernice E. Young, Los Angeles

VI
In the Back Country

San Diego's remarkably varied and beautiful countryside has inspired some of the best regional writing in the West. The pieces that follow represent a half century of back country impressions—from Willard Wood's lyrical sketch of a motor trip through the Warner Ranch country, to Judy Van der Veer's sensitive portrait of old Santa Ysabel, to Russ Leadabrand's more recent prose poem on the spell of San Diego county names. During the 1930s, '40s and '50s Westways regularly published articles by two gifted and energetic writers, Philip Johnston and Farnsworth Crowder. Johnston probably knew California and the Southwestern U.S. as well, if not better, than any man alive; and Farnsworth's clever and gently satiric "Escondido" is typical of a number of town portraits he did for the magazine.

A Back Country Idyll

Willard Wood

For miles after leaving the smooth concrete of the Inland Route to San Diego at Temecula we had followed the vagrant wanderings of a seemingly irresponsible road. It had dipped through sandy washes, climbed narrow canyons, cooled our tires with the water of strange streams. At Oak Grove it invited us to rest under giant oaks, and refresh our eyes with the sight of green fields and grazing cattle. The ancient stage station, built eighty years ago, reminded us that the road was old enough to have acquired wisdom, no matter how youthful and foolish it seemed. Then beyond Oak Grove we climbed again till a sharper touch in the air told of the altitude we had reached. And presently, instead of climbing, the road dropped away to the east through a grassy meadow, fringed with cottonwoods, that seemed somehow to mark the boundary of a new country. Not a modern country either, for we remembered that in thirty miles we had not encountered a single motor car nor seen half a dozen houses.

The sun dropped and the shadow of the hills overtook us, when suddenly at dusk we emerged into a vast open, grassy valley. Thousands of cattle grazed far and near but there was no sign of human life. The road skirted the edge of the valley, and on a high green knoll that rose to the left of the road was outlined against a darkening sky the half ruined walls of an ancient adobe.

Puerta la Cruz it was—"Door of the Cross," on the rancho of Saint Joseph of the Valley—the great Warner ranch in northeastern San Diego county. It was too dark to see in the valley below the giant pear and apple trees that were set out when the adobe was built long ago. On the very tracks that our rubber tires pressed once passed the iron-shod wheels of the famous Butterfield line—the ruined adobe walls had doubtless sheltered its passengers. And, coming upon it as we did in the half light, the whole scene carried a vivid impression that we had somehow motored back through the years, and come unawares upon the old California.

It is an impression that has never really left me, and one that lends never-failing charm to the excursions that I have made to the "back country" of San Diego county. The back country of San Diego county is to me a sort of precious museum where I can go now and then and observe California in its natural state, minus all the improvements of a modern civilization. Concrete highways are splendid things, but it is pleasant none the less to feel a dirt road once in a while under your tires. It is pleasant, too, to find a building that the mission fathers built whose corridors have never echoed the whistle of a locomotive, nor the jangle of a trolley bell. San Gabriel, Santa Barbara, San Juan Capistrano, Ventura—all of these missions the tide of an alien civilization has engulfed so thoroughly that their charm is well nigh gone. But Pala, low-roofed, dreaming Pala, with the white campanile rising from the *campo santo* beside the chapel—that is another story. The campanile, by the way, is the only structure of its sort among all the buildings constructed by the Franciscans. It is a copy of the campanile of the old church in Juarez, Mexico, built in 1549.

But to be a little more specific, what are the things worth seeing in San Diego's back country, and how is the best way to see them? Well, here is a list: Oak Grove; Warner Hot Springs; Montezuma Valley and the view of the desert; Santa Ysabel and the ancient mission bells; Julian, "the lost town of Julian;" Mesa Grande and Powam Lodge; Pine Hills; Witch Creek; Pala; Palomar Mountain; and Amago and the winding road that follows the San Luis Rey. It is a list that you cannot include in one trip, or in two, and see them all rightly. For myself, I even have times and seasons for the different places. Warner's Hot Springs, though attractive at other seasons, is at its very best in late springtime when the vast rancho is a rippling sea of green, shot through with wild flowers, and when there is a meadow lark on every fencepost for your delight. The little adobe houses at Warner's are perfectly suited to carry out the illusion of the California of the past, and it is to be hoped that they never will be replaced with any more modern structures.

Then, too, the morning chorus of birds in the white locust trees at Warner's is something to remember if you visit there in the full tide of the spring. Many of our Southern California birds are migrants, coming up from Mexico in the spring. Warner's is almost at the summit of the divide, and just to the eastward lies the great Colorado desert. Over its hundreds of desolate, terrible miles, the tiny songsters have come—to a land of trees, of water and green grass and soft breezes. To hear them in the dawn in the trees at Warner's, you can well believe the birds rejoicing that their desert journey is done.

If you are curious to see a world as different as day is from night, leave Warner's and take the Montezuma Valley road to the point that overlooks the Colorado Desert to the east. It looks a land of death—no less. The Salton Sea, a turquoise set in dull copper, lies below you. Beyond, illimitable wastes of dun desert, then the desolate, barren Chocolate Mountains.

Though Pine Hills is a famous summer resort, and the tiny houses in the trees uniquely charming of summer nights, yet it is the fall of the year that suits me best to visit the Julian country. For Julian is an apple country, and apple growers of Julian have not yet learned the gentle art of profiteering. Likewise they press cider there that is the real juice of the apple—not the vile imitations full of embalming fluid that you buy at the roadside stands near Los Angeles. . . .

Palomar Mountain—that is the trip to make in full midsummer. Out to Temecula, over Pala Grande after leaving the Inland road, and up the valley of the San Luis Rey for half a dozen winding miles. Then the Palomar road turns sharply to the left and the climb begins. The south slope of Palomar is barren and hot, and gives not the slightest hint of the beauty of the summit. But, once at the top, you come suddenly into the trees—the most beautiful forest in Southern California, in my judgment. Gigantic black oaks, cedar, and fir clothe Palomar's summit with a majesty that is not equaled anywhere else in this comparatively treeless land. . . . Along the five thousand foot summit of the mountain the road winds, and below is spread a life-size contour map of most of San Diego County. Clear nights you may see the harbor lights of San Diego; days, when the sea mist is swept away, the headlands of the lonely Coronado Islands lift from the blue sea rim. Southeast, range after range of tumbled mountains melt into one another till the desolate Cocopahs of Lower California form the last faint blue line.

Years ago there were more settlers on Palomar's summit than there are today. At least, if you seek, you will find to the north of Bailey's, which is the resort on the summit, a tiny red schoolhouse tucked away under the trees. The children are gone from Palomar now—for years the schoolhouse has been tenantless. A lithograph of McKinley and Hobart on the walls inside will tell you perhaps the date of its abandonment.

But here is a word of warning, by way of closing. If you are of that class of motorist whose sole enjoyment lies in the number of miles you can record on your speedometer in a day's travel, do not visit the back country of San Diego county. It is a leisurely land—it should be traveled leisurely. Its dirt roads are for the most part splendid to travel, save in the rainy season, but if it is your sole pride to average thirty miles an hour, why, stay away, for you won't enjoy yourself. If the color and romance of California's history mean nothing to you, half the charm of those historic roads and valleys will be empty. But to those who really love the outdoors, and especially the California outdoors, there is a real empire of enjoyment waiting for you in the back country of San Diego County.

(1920)

The Lure of the Lagunas
Philip Johnston

One of the strangest paradoxes in Southern California is found on the margin of the Colorado Desert. It is a high plateau, crowned with a dense forest of pine, juniper, and live oak; a wild botanical garden ablaze with floral colors; a sylvan retreat that seems to have been made to order for heat-harried denizens of the wilderness to the east, and of low-lying valleys to the west.

Such are the Laguna Mountains in eastern San Diego County. Taking root in the simmering wasteland, their barren, rock-buttressed slopes have frowned upon many a race that has become dust; have looked down upon the plodding ox-wagons of Lieutenant Colonel Philip St. George Cooke with his Mormon Battalion; have yielded treasure in gold only to see its finder plundered and slain.

There seems to be a strange inconsistency in the story of these mountains. In days long forgotten, the valleys about them saw human deeds that were dark, and witnessed the savage resistance offered by the wilderness to temerarious travelers. Yet their wooded heights, cool and alluring, laved by springs and lush with grass and wild flowers, offered a delightful sanctuary to red men long before the white wings of Cabrillo's ship rode over the blue horizon far to the west.

Sky-piercing, umbrageous, the dark pines now whisper to scores of campers; whisper of times within the memory of living men when this was a forest primeval; when moccasined feet glided over pine needles where rubber-tired vehicles now roll. For Indian sway was broken suddenly, dramatically, three score years ago in a one-sided battle. Gazing backward in retreat, the aborigines saw the smoke of their homes mounting skyward; saw the menacing muzzles of rifles, and continued their flight. All physical trace of that tragedy has vanished; but the story has survived in a name given to the glade where it occurred—*Burnt Ranchería.*

It was some time later that a compassionate government set aside two small tracts as reservations; but today, the need for them has all but passed. The Cuyapaipe Reservation has barely a dozen inhabitants, and the Laguna Reservation is tenanted by the last lone survivor of a once-powerful clan.

Today, the Lagunas are acclaimed among the most delightful of all recreation areas below the Tehachapi.

And the region's natural charm is enhanced by its easy access, for it lies only eleven miles from the Imperial Valley Highway, and the intervening grades are so gentle as to offer no impediment to the most asthmatic flivver. Discovered and highly appreciated by scores of vacationists, it still remains the sparsest human population of any similar place in the southland. . . .

Remarkable as a playground, there are other features of the Laguna Mountains of more than passing interest to the visitor. Half a mile from the ranger station is Desert Rim, to which a car may be driven, which affords a breath-taking view of the wilderness one mile below and spread out to a far horizon like a giant relief map. In the middle distance, one may discern the Salton Sea, a lake of blue against a tawny background. Another memorable glimpse of the desert may be had from Vallecito View, three miles from the ranger station, where a lofty watchtower has been constructed around a gnarled pine. But the climactic experience of a visit to this eyrie is found on Monument Peak, that rises to an altitude of 6321 feet. . . .

Wheeling about and facing the Pacific, one is even more astounded by the view spread out before him. Plainly discernible, the city of San Diego edges close to its landlocked bay, while beyond, the blue ocean describes a giant arc against the skyline. Upon a clear day, the San Clemente Island may be seen, dim and tenuous in the distance.

Appalling in their grandeur, the views from Monument Peak are never to be forgotten; but far more interest attaches to the narrow desert valley below its northern slope. It was here that historic dramas were played when the West was young.

Desert-worn, distraught, their animals fatigued to the point of exhaustion, soldiers under command of General Stephen W. Kearny toiled over that sandy route in December, 1846. Their quest was another star for Old Glory's galaxy. Awaiting them in the brush-clad uplands toward the sea were the rough-riding vaqueros led by Andrés Pico, who were to administer, a few days later, the only major reverse suffered by American arms in the conquest of California.

A few weeks later, Lieutenant Colonel Cooke with his Mormon Battalion piloted the first wagons over this route. Sure-footed mules and cavalry mounts had already followed ancient trails made by the Indians, but the broad-gauged vehicles were stopped by the precipitous walls of Box Canyon. It was only by the hardest of labor with picks, axes, and shovels that the intrepid band was able to hew a road through the gorge—and not one of the toilers dreamed that he was forging a link in a transcontinental road.

Thirteen years later, stages of the Butterfield Overland Mail were careening over the desert road flanking Carrizo Creek. With a brief pause at Vallecito to change horses—and to permit passengers to lave the dust of travel from their throats at the tiny bar—they continued over the tortuous road through Yuma, across the wasteland of Southern Arizona, and on to St. Louis. . . .

A soft voice is heard today over the summit of Laguna Mountain. It is that sibilant, alluring whisper of massed pines—an obligato for the gay songsters that build their nests among swaying branches. There is beauty, too, in the myriads of wild flowers that cover the ground in springtime—stands of evening primrose; brilliant dashes of red Indian paintbrush and scarlet Pentstemon; stately blue flax, and that curious bloom called golden eardrops. All of these seem to have been made to order for an ever-growing throng of nature lovers and recreation seekers.

(1935)

Memories of Julian

Horace Fenton Wilcox
(as told to John Edwin Hogg)

Minin' camps is like toadstools. They spring up overnight, so to speak; then, when the pay dirt's gone, they usually blow up higher'n a kite. The miners, saloon keepers, gamblers, painted ladies, merchants, and all the rest it takes to make up a minin' camp such as Julian was in the '70s, load out like rats gettin' clear of a sinkin' ship. That's been the story of minin' camps 'most everywhere. But Julian's different. It sprouted right out of these mountains as a minin' camp. It boomed for about ten years and busted like the one-hoss shay. After that it staged a come-back. Now it's a fine little town with a wonderful future.

I came to Julian on June 11, 1872, when Julian was a rag-house minin' town, an' goin' strong. I was twenty-eight years old then. I've been here ever since, and havin' been here nearly sixty years, I'm one of the oldest residents of the community. I'm also one of the few old-timers left that was here durin' the gold rush. . . .

We hadn't been in Julian very long before father's mines turned out to be just plain holes in the ground, and somethin' had to be done to help the family income. We was a musical family. I used to play the bass viol, and father was a fiddler. I found work now and then as a musician, while father had a fairly steady job fiddlin' in the dance halls. But my health was so bad then I wasn't much of a success as a musician. I'd usually manage to get a chill right in the middle of every dance number, and I'd shake. When this happened my bass viol sounded like a hoot owl. The dancers would fall all over each others' feet tryin' to keep time with my chills and music.

I had to find some sort of work that my health would let me do, and music and saw mills was about the only things I knew. There was a man by the name of William Shaw who'd set up a saw mill just outside of Julian. . . . One day I went to see him, and begged him for a job until he put me to work. I worked for him for $2 a day for five years.

The George Washington Mine was the original mine in the Julian district. It was discovered by Frank Gorman, a thirteen-year-old boy, the oldest of four children of the Gorman family. These people, with two other families, the Skidmores and the Ragsdales, was wagonin' through with oxen from San Antonio, Texas, to San Diego. They was tom-turkey poor, and had had a terrible time comin' across the desert country to the east. When they got up here where Julian is now, their animals was in such bad shape they decided to make camp to re-condition their oxen and rest up a bit.

The Gorman boy had heard a lot of talk about gold in California, and he began lookin' for it as soon as the party got across the Colorado River from Arizona. While camped in Pine Valley one day, Frank was sent out to bring in some firewood. He walked to where a big oak tree had fallen down, and while gettin' the wood he noticed some white rocks with yellow specks. He took a chunk of the rock back to his father and the stuff was soon identified as very rich gold ore. The elder Gorman immediately staked out his claim, which turned out to be one of the richest mines ever developed in the Julian district. Because this strike was made on February 22, 1870, Washington's birthday, they called it the George Washington Mine. Millions was taken out of it.

With the discovery of the George Washington Mine, the Julian gold rush was on. Men poured in from everywhere and plenty other places. New mines were located nearly every day. Soon after the real rush began, a man by the name of Drew Bailey filed a homestead, and laid out a town at the north end of the valley. A miners' meetin' was called to outline the camp, give it a name, and organize a town gover'ment. They elected Mike Julian as recorder, and named the place Julian after him. I staked out a lot of claims myself, but the more mines I owned, the poorer I got.

After quittin' Shaw I went up to Banner and went to work as a bookkeeper for Louis Cohen. Cohen was a fine fellow, and had a wonderful store in Banner. He carried a great stock of liquors and merchandise, and was makin' money in heaps. But he was a terrible drinker—a reg'lar human sponge for whiskey. Whiskey ruined him. He was seldom sober, and eventually he drank himself to death. He died with the horrors! Whiskey was the curse of all these early minin' camps, and Julian was no different from the rest. I saw no less than seventy-five men drink themselves to death the first year I was here.

Durin' the gold rush Julian and Banner was pretty tough places, but I reckon they wasn't any tougher'n most minin' camps of that time. Every other place of business was a saloon, a gamblin' joint, or a dance hall; but on the whole things was pretty orderly. We never had much shootin'. There was no stealin'. Respectable women was perfectly safe, and people in general was a lot more honest and trustworthy than they are now'days.

Legal justice was swift and sure. Criminals didn't come into court with a staff of trick lawyers like they do now.

To give you an idea how crime was treated, we had one terrible case here about 1874. It called for a hangin', and the party that was due to get his neck stretched got it stretched quick. This fellow—somehow my mind slips down on his name so let's call him Juan López for tellin' the story—attacked a white woman, the wife of a miner. López had gone up to Banner early one mornin' and got full of whiskey. On the way back to Julian he met the white woman with a very small baby in her arms comin' along the trail. He attacked her, stabbed her, and left her for dead. Ten minutes after this crime was discovered a town meetin' was called, and a reward of $50 offered for Juan López, dead or alive.

We had a constable here then, and he was a Yaqui Indian from Mexico. Ambrosia Ruíz was his name, and Ambrosia could track down anything on feet or hoofs that ever tried to move through this part of the country. He immediately took up the trail from the scene of the crime, and like a bloodhound tracked his man over the mountains and down into the desert. In the desert Ruíz trailed his man north for about ten miles where he had followed the contours along the foot of the mountains. There the trail turned into a canyon, and about two miles up the canyon went into an Indian camp. Ambrosia saw the man had gone into the camp, and hadn't come out.

Findin' the head man of the Indians, Ambrosia backed him against the side of a shack at the point of two revolvers. Speakin' in Spanish, which was the language all the Indians around here understood, he told him what had happened at Julian. "I'm here to get that man," said Ambrosia. "Now bring him out. If you try to hide him every white man in Julian will be down here. They'll kill every last Indian of you, and burn your camp." It didn't take the Indians very long to deliver the prisoner, securely bound, and mounted on a horse. Then they sent a runner straight over the mountains to take the word to Julian that Ambrosia would soon be there with the prisoner.

When Ambrosia got to Julian everything was ready. A grave had been dug. A big rock had been pulled up with a rope over the limb of an oak tree. The other end of the rope was adjusted around the prisoner's neck. Then the rock came down, and López went up danglin' by the neck. In due time he was cut down and buried with his boots on. There was no more of that sort of crime around Julian.

The strangest part of this story is that the woman in the case recovered. Despite the most terrible injuries —more than thirty knife wounds—she lingered between life and death for weeks, and then began to get well. She's still wearin' the scars, although she's a very old woman now, and livin' not far from here. It would be best not to mention her name.

After I'd worked for Cohen for a time I got a charter to build a toll road from Julian to Banner. Banner was then producin' more gold than Julian, and there was no way to get at it except by pack train until my brothers, my father, and I, built the road. This toll road turned out to be a profitable financial venture for us.

While workin' on the toll road one day, two of my brothers and I got in on the prelude of one of the few shootin' scrapes that Julian ever had that resulted in a man bein' killed.

A Mexican by the name of Jesús Garcia drifted into Banner one day. He was apparently an educated and well-to-do fellow. At least, he spoke good English, and had a good horse, good saddle, and two silver-plated six-guns. He went into Ike Levy's saloon in Banner, asked for whiskey, and took several drinks. Levy had set the bottle on the bar, and Garcia, after helpin' himself to as many drinks as he wanted, refused to pay for them. This resulted in the Mexican bein' chased out of town, and he came down the road toward Julian to where we was workin'. The minute he saw us he began to threaten us with his guns, and cussed us out for everything he could lay his tongue to. Bein' unarmed we wasn't inclined to argue with him. So we run up the hill and hid behind a combin' of rocks until the Mexican got tired and went away. He went on down the road into Julian.

In Julian, Garcia went into the Silver Dollar saloon, pulled his guns on Frank Hopkins, the barkeeper, and demanded whiskey. Frank set the bottle on the bar and said: "There you are, stranger. Help yourself." Garcia, of course, had to lay one of his guns down on the bar to pour a drink. Watchin' him like a hawk, Hopkins wiggled along the bar to a place where he kept a gun on a shelf under the bar. Then, as the Mexican started to pour the drink, the barkeeper grabbed his gun and fired. Garcia fell dead, drilled through the heart, as all the other saloon patrons flattened out on the floor.

Hopkins then walked out of the saloon and across the street to the coroner's office. Speakin' to the officer, he said: "I just killed a man in self-defense over in the Silver Dollar. You better come over and hold an inquest." So, the inquest was held in the saloon. Hopkins was exonerated and given a vote of thanks for havin' rid the community of a dangerous person. They carried the Mexican out and buried him. . . .

I realize that I've limped along all these years to become a very old man. My life has been mostly years of suffering. Now that I'm so ruinously old, I'm practically broke. But what of it? What would I do with money if I had it? As I look back over my life, what

changes I've seen! I still get a thrill out of watchin'
it, and I wouldn't have missed it for anything, even to
escape the tortures of this battered old body of mine.
My requirements of life are now two meals a day and
a good bed. If I had all the gold coin that was ever taken
out of the Julian district I'd have no more use for it
than I'd have for a hundred silk hats.

(1932)

Escondido—Middletown in California

Farnsworth Crowder

Escondido is a Spanish word meaning "hidden"; Escondido is a river and a valley ("the sunkis't vale");
Escondido is a town of 3421 souls (1930 census) in
northeastern San Diego County; and Escondido is a
demonstration, ingenuous and candid, of how California
can infect sober immigrants from the American mid-
lands with the psychology of a chamber of commerce
secretary and the enthusiasms of a pastoral poet.

Zeal appeared with the group of gringo entrepreneurs
who founded the settlement just over a half century ago.
And small wonder: for think of being able to buy up
12,000 acres of "the Garden Spot of the Earth," "the
Eden of the Western Hemisphere," with "the most
equable climate in the world" at only $5 an acre, and
then turn it around and offer it in farm tracts and town
lots to Hawkeyes and Hoosiers, weary of chilblains
and blizzards, for from ten to fifty times that much!

However well *escondido* may have described the valley as being "hidden," it did not suit it as a real estate project. There was no hankering for isolation in the bosoms of those early city fathers anxious to turn their money. They stood up, as it were, on the summit of Palomar Mountain and clarioned off toward the Mississippi:

"You folks back east who have laid around rotten old boroughs so long that you have become stagnated, come to Escondido and breathe the pure air of energy and catch the spirit of pluck, and in a few years go back to your wife's people with a pocket full of wealth and a body full of health."

When this summons appeared (1886), along with five columns of advertising and a batch of touching poetry—*Mother's Love* and *To the Apple*—on the front page of the *Escondido Times,* the town was but five months old and contained only 300 inhabitants. It was nevertheless boasting thirty businesses and a 100-room hotel, was holding out prospects of fine fruit without irrigation, laying plans for Escondido College, erecting a public school and a Methodist Church, promising a railroad, and, through the *Times,* was even telling the city of Los Angeles where to get off; advising those absurd people up there to quit trying to make a harbor out of an old slough that had been lying around for centuries and realize they would have to depend on San Diego Bay.

Well, the fine fruit without irrigation didn't grow; the college did not materialize; the streetcar line built out Grand Avenue from the depot never ran but one car over its tracks; some of the early comers, hearkening to the call to "See Escondido and Live," were skinned out of their shirts by sharp practices on the part of land dealers and bankers. But vicissitudes did no worse than embarrass Escondido in the fulfillment of its destiny.

Imagine the palms, eucalypti, and peppers cleared

away and the encircling mountains leveled down. Then imagine a family of expectant arrivals from rural Ohio looking for a new home in the promised land. Picture them driving into Escondido along North Broadway, circling the flagpole at the intersection with Grand Avenue and pulling up for a look around. They blink and they wonder, with a slight sickness about the diaphragm, if they have not traveled in a 2000-mile circle, right back to where they started from. Because everything looks so familiar. The brick and stone façades, the show windows along Grand Avenue's business blocks might be duplicated in any number of Ohio valley towns. Humpty Dumpty's Complete Food Store, with the Eagles' Hall upstairs, might have come right along with them from back home. Ting's Pharmacy, diagonally across the corner, could be Ingvolstad's Drug store on Main Street back in Plunketville.

Except for an occasional loitering Mexican, the people on the sidewalks look like the folks at home—which is as it should be, since that is where most of them came from.

Let our hypothetical family cruise about a little, south from Grand toward High School hill. The streets bear no exotic Hispanic or Indian names—just prosaic *Second, Third, Fourth* and so on in one direction, *Hickory, Ivy, Juniper* and *Maple* in the other. The dwellings are modest, old-fashioned frame houses with shingled roofs and awkward gables. The new Union High School is sensible brick and stone. No mission-bell lamp posts, no Indian-pueblo gift shops, no Spanish arcades, no exquisite campanile gracing the post office, no neo-California nonsense anywhere. It is all a bit disappointing.

That they may see the valley as a map, let our Ohio family ride out West Grand, past the Mexican settlement and the depot and turn up to Mr. and Mrs. Dan Hankins' Hotel Charlotta, standing in the midst of rich hill top orchards. It is said of The Charlotta that it was built by a transplanted Chicagoan whose house was so everlastingly infested with vacationists from back east that, partly to be accommodating and partly in self-defense, he put up a hotel for his friends. It is quite as homey and informal as that story would imply. From its rambling second-story balcony the newcomers can look out on town and valley.

No, this is not rural Ohio after all. To be sure it is agricultural; it is nothing else but. The district has scarcely a dime of manufacturing income. Its basic $4,000,000 annual receipts derive from the soil. But not in the shape of grain and hogs. $2,000,000 is from the acres planted to citrus. The broad, flat building visible through the trees west of town is the lemon-packing house. The other two sheds, north along the Santa Fe tracks, handle the orange pick.

Though the lowly hen makes no such spectacular show on the landscape as do the vineyards, the avocado and walnut groves, she is much more important, accounting for the second largest item of income—almost $1,000,000. The dairy cow does somewhat better than half as well as the hen, while grapes, avocados, walnuts, deciduous fruits, vegetables and hay are, in the aggregate, about as productive as madam cow.

If Escondido were to adopt a crest, it could hardly refrain from a quartered shield bearing a lemon, a white leghorn rooster, a milk can and a bunch of grapes.

And what does this countryside productiveness mean to the town? For one thing, with citrus prices holding up so well, with no factories or mines to close down and no tourist catering enterprises to fold up, Escondido was one of the communities in California to suffer least from depression. For another—despite the way folks run down to shop in the big stores in San Diego—Escondido does a larger per capita retail business than any city in Southern California except Taft.

In short it is, beside being beautiful to look upon, a pretty substantial setup, worth our home-seeker's consideration. And Escondido loves home-seekers, especially if they are white, native-born American, and fairly affluent.

But you needn't tell this to Pansy Claggett. She is the rushing hearty secretary of the Chamber of Commerce, runs a fruit ranch of her own, gets up the stunning exhibits at State and County fairs that have won Escondido twenty-three firsts out of twenty-five attempts, and knows everybody from the first families such as the Whalfords and Turrentines to the Filipino boys that the Sunkist people keep in residence to pick lemons, because they don't mind a soaking in the wet foliage and can scramble about like monkeys in the trees.

Our home-seeker can find Miss Claggett by driving down to the Chamber of Commerce at the corner of Maple and Grand. Edna Hill, the gracious, pretty little brunette who works for the Automobile Club, can point him to Pansy's office—clearing-house extraordinary for all the community's gossip, tribulations, schemes, and civic enterprises. Just now we shall have to wait for big Johnnie Johnson to finish bluing the air over the "amateur" government inspectors who keep messing around his winery.

When it comes our home-seeker's turn he must expect a warm hand and an earful. She will tell him how ideally Escondido can fulfill his dream of owning a productive little tract in California. She will explain that the local farm bureau is the liveliest and most helpful in the state; and she is about right. She will tell him how many lodges, societies, service clubs and churches there are to make him welcome. She will remind him that he will be a neighbor to Harold Bell Wright, the valley's most famed citizen, and its quietest philanthropist. And when she has finished her story and answered his questions, she will take our prospective settler out in the other room and introduce him to Mr. England, the agricultural inspector, who will set him straight on matters pertaining to land, water rights and crops.

And now he is ready for the Land and Town Company people or for some good realtor like Claude Wilson. The Land and Town Company is the concern that set things going fifty years ago by buying up what had been originally a Spanish grant, Rancho *Rincon del Diablo* ("Lurking Place of the Devil"), laying out a town, building the hotel, giving land to churches and schools, petitioning the Santa Fe for a railroad spur, installing a water system and inviting the world to come and settle.

Our home-seeker can get good undeveloped land for $350 per acre. Or he can buy a flourishing orchard for a whole lot more than that. Like most people he will take only ten to twenty acres. Escondido is not a rich man's corner. There are several well-to-do and a good many who are comfortably fixed; but there is no millionaire's row. The most flashy thing in the way of buildings is an Indian tepee sixty feet high, built by an Idaho sheepman on a prominent valley hilltop.

Father will have to buy enough Class A shares in the Mutual Water Company to assure him a supply for irrigation. He will join the Lemon Association and one or other of the orange houses. He will be invited to one of the bi-monthly meetings of the Chamber of Commerce to get introduced to the big-shots of the community, and he will be smart to accept. He will tie up with the Farm Bureau and make use of the excellent services of the agricultural inspectors.

He will drive to town some morning to acquaint himself with the tractor and implement lines at Spencer &

McFarlane's huge place on North Broadway and to order a supply of chicken feed from Gordon Howell. At noon, to tide him over, he can get a de luxe hamburger at Squeak's on the alley or walk up the street to Jordan's for the merchants' lunch. He will get to know Jordan's pretty well, because all sorts of groups make use of the special dining room.

He will open an account at the Security Trust or the Bank of America. Both are branch institutions so that Escondido is deprived of that awesome, storybook figure —the town banker. Other chain institutions—Penney, Safeway, and Piggly Wiggly—have cut in on home-cured business.

On down Grand, beyond the two-by-four city hall and police station, Father can stop in at the offices of the daily *Times-Advocate* to enter his subscription. The staff of three, including Editor-Publisher Percy Evans, will possibly be at their tiny desks knocking out copy on ancient Olivers and Royals while out back rumbles the press once used by the *Los Angeles Express*. It came around the Horn in the days before there was a railroad into Los Angeles and it still rolls out excellent type six days a week.

Arrangements will have to be made for getting the children in school. The two younger ones can be picked up and returned daily in one of the big, bright-yellow schoolbuses. With the community growing so fast in the 'twenties and depression tightening purse-strings in the 'thirties, the elementary school is overcrowded, but enough parents are becoming exercised about it that in due time there will be a new building comparable to Union High, the handsomest thing in town.

Fred, who finished the twelfth grade last year, can commute back and forth to the junior college at Oceanside. Most Escondido youngsters who go off to college never come back to stay. The cities get them. Those who quit with high school are more inclined to remain at home, marry a schoolgirl sweetheart and settle down.

Sister, who wants neither to go to college nor stick around the house as a "home-girl," rustles herself a job clerking at the Escondido Mercantile, so that she can meet people and be seen, go out for lunch with other girls at the Chat 'n Chew or Rolfe's fountain and perhaps interest a fellow who will like taking a pretty blonde to the movies at the Pala and squiring her to potluck suppers and dances.

For reasons social, business and religious, the whole family will want to have their church letters transferred. There are seventeen flourishing churches in town. Escondido is essentially a community of good, salt-of-the-earth people who are little troubled by modern heresies and have no sympathy with the revolt of the angels. The Congregationalists, with their fine Pilcher pipe organ and their new Plymouth Hall providing Sunday school quarters and a big social hall, are rather out in the lead. For the summer, friendly rivalries are retired for the benefit of the union services held in the park.

Father will doutbless find a chapter of his lodge. If he has a passion for golf, there is a country club. There is no social hurdle to membership; the club does not constitute "a set." It is amazingly heterogeneous and the public is welcome at the five or six big functions of the year; because the exchequer needs the cash.

The Woman's Club will get around to giving Mother a bid. With its bungalow clubhouse occupying the same square with the Carnegie Library, it stands at the cultural heart of the town. It is duly conscientious about interspersing bridge parties, dances and teas with musicals and literary sessions. The regular meetings of the book section are really formidable affairs. They take up in the forenoon with some clever woman like Mrs. Amos Peek reviewing six or seven works, from fiction through biography to economics. At noon, the ladies knock off for the hostess committee to serve luncheon, after which Miss Ethel Creigh of the county library staff carries on into the afternoon with a report on another half dozen books.

The requirements for admission to these Escondido circles and activities would seem to be literacy, a clean face and a disposition to be friendly and coöperative. One can circulate comfortably from top to bottom of the social structure without wealth, pedigree or a dress suit. There are people who make a try at crashing the upper layers in San Diego, but at home in the valley putting on airs yields slim satisfaction.

There are facilities and machinery to keep the family entertained in off hours. Across the river from the Grape Day Park is a diamond equipped for night baseball. The season extends almost around the calendar and there are few things that tickle the citizens more than watching Karl Hoffman of the Escondidans chucking great ball against a rival club.

The park provides a plunge, horseshoe pits and a new adobe shell where Director Stoddard's town band holds forth with summer Sunday concerts. For night life in the modern cocktail manner there is only one "spot"— the Barn. Those who must have metropolitan atmosphere to enjoy themselves can drive the thirty-four miles to San Diego.

In summer when the hot days come, the Pacific is available an hour away. The mountains are always patiently there for picnicking and motoring, for fishing and hunting, in season.

Escondido has fifty-three big communal moments a year: the fifty-two that occur each Saturday, P.M., when everybody drives in to shop, visit, "eat out" and, in the evening, to see a show or a ball game or go to a dance; the fifty-third comes annually on Admission

Day, the 9th of September. This supreme moment assumes the proportions of a county fair, with as many as 20,000 visitors. . . .

The celebration is off with a gala parade down Grand Avenue. All day in and about the park something is going on, bands playing, speakers raving, amateur athletes straining their joints, children getting lost, flirtations breaking out and the inevitable ball players smacking out home runs—while twenty tons of free sun-sweet muscats vanish bunch by bunch. Dancing climaxes everything—on canvas stretched in the park, on the huge floor of the west side Co-op building, at the Eagles' Hall and on the sidewalks. . . .

Escondidans talk hopefully of luring more tourist trade, of developing their gold lode and their clay banks, of Thelma Clark's proposed dude ranch on her big 4 S property and of what the Caltech observatory on Palomar Mountain will do for them. But such things are really incidentals, on the margin; it is the red sandy soil that will always be Escondido's old reliable.

Give our Ohio family a few good seasons on their bit of that soil and you will begin to detect the symptoms of a case of California zeal.

Probably, some year, when things are slack between the Valencia and Navel harvests, the family will drive back to Ohio. And Father, strutting before his wife's people, showing off his body full of health, will break out indiscreetly: "Say, listen, you folks back East here, lying around this rotten old borough so long you've stagnated, why don't you come out to Escondido and breathe the pure air of energy and catch the spirit of pluck? Now, for instance, let me tell you about my Red Emperor grapes. And say, the wild lilacs on the hills in spring, all white and lavender—"

(1937)

The Minnesota Skeptic—
A Murray Lake Fish Story

Joe Mears

Where had I seen that familiar gleam? That "Now I've got you over a barrel" look; that sort of combination of the exultant smirk of a poker player who's got aces up when he knows you've only got kings; and the maddening, self-satisfied grin of a Dizzy Dean facing a .150 hitter with three on and two down!

Not that I didn't have it coming. I'd sketched, in my usual conservative way, the few outstanding attractions Southern California had to offer my newly-arrived tourist friend from Minnesota, here to take in the San Diego World's Fair [of 1935] and any other attractions lying around loose. I'd been modest but the list was, I suppose, rather long. Finally I came to fishing, which is my favorite subject, now that I'm getting along in years. Then I saw that mocking, half-derisive look in his pale blue eyes.

"Fishing?" His tone was annoying. "Well, I'll concede your tackle-busting steelheads, your Sierran rainbows and goldens and your savage lake trout offer sport that compares with the average run-of-the-mill fishing we have in Minnesota. But, pray tell, what have you to offer in the way of fresh-water bass fishing?"

As a Hollywood wit would doubtless say: "Was that a challenge or *was* it a challenge?" I was well aware, painfully so, of his prowess as a fisherman. Stuffed bass, muskies, lake trout, etc., etc., on the walls of his den. Also, he'd fished for the matchless steelheads of the

Klamath, Eel, Rogue and Umpqua. But he'd never cast a bass plug in California water. Until I was willing to be the victim, he'd never heard there were any bass in California.

"Oh, you've got large-mouths, all right," he said, in a feeble attempt at humor. "But not the finny kind."

Through the early morning high fog we felt our way down the coast highway, past Laguna Beach. Stopping for ham and eggs at San Diego, we headed the prow of our equipage toward University Avenue about ten miles to the quiet, homelike city of La Mesa. There, by prior arrangements, we picked up Rube and Luther, bass fishermen par excellence. You see, I wasn't taking any chances.

Shortly we were at Murray Lake. With true San Diego County hospitality, Rube had previously arranged to have our boat equipped with his outboard. Rube took his place in the stern and made an excellent skipper. We agreed only two of us would fish at one time, to avoid hooking somebody's hat, or worse.

Charley's smile broadened as we putt-putted along the reed-lined shore. "Looks like good bass water to me," he opined, drawing upon his Minnesota knowledge. "And that little ripple won't hurt anything. Let's get going."

Rube anchored the boat in a small cove, so that within radius of seventy-five or 100 feet we had plenty of good casting water.

Charley rigged up his casting rod before any of us. From the depths of his gigantic tackle box he produced a battered red-headed plug and tied it on his line. His first few casts, with an ease and distance that marked him as an expert, brought admiring comment from Luther and Rube but failed to net any bass.

"Good practice, anyway," said Charley. "So. . . ."

Readers of fishing yarns expect the climax to come when the dub of the party lands the biggest fish of the day. Or when the author has proved, against overwhelming odds, some statement he made at the outset. Our present story conforms to the conventional pattern both to the extent that our cynical Swedish friend, a novice at California bass fishing, should snag the biggest bronzeback of the trip at Murray Lake; also in that our good luck, the writer fondly hopes, establishes the fact that there is good bass fishing in San Diego County under average conditions.

Charley was a good scout and agreed I was right about California bass fishing. In fact he was all for staying a week. Such being impossible for me, due to the fact that I wasn't on vacation from Minnesota, Charley suggested that we check up on conditions in all the San Diego lakes, for future reference.

"You get a week off in July," he urged, "and we'll come down, do the fair from cover to cover, and make the rounds of the lakes. If the two close-in reservoirs are a sample there ought to be some honest-to-goodness fishing in some of the more remote spots."

(1935)

The Valley of Santa Ysabel
Judy Van der Veer

Of all beautiful little valleys, my favorite is Santa Ysabel, which lies between Ramona and Julian, about fifty-two miles northeast of San Diego and seven miles northwest of Julian. The view of it from Highway 79 is, I think, one of the gentlest views in all California. There are rolling meadows, gracious with live oaks, and mountains rising tall in the background. The sun shines on the red roof of the chapel and its pure white walls; horses and cattle move in the meadows. It is very easy to whiz right by the combined store and post office, and start the climb to Julian without realizing what a wonderful place is being left behind. A left turn, instead of going toward Julian, leads to Mesa Grande, Lake Henshaw, Warner's Hot Springs, or Palomar Mountain.

This valley, beloved by Indians, has always interested me, partly because of its beauty and partly because it has a fascinating history—and it has a secret.

Santa Ysabel was a grant of 17,719.40 acres, having originally belonged to the San Diego Mission. The early missionary priests, Father Mariner in 1795, and Fathers Payeras and Sanchez in 1821, were impressed by the large population of Indians, and more impressed by the fact that the Indians seemed unusually intelligent. An adobe chapel was built; by 1822 there was a granary, several houses, a cemetery and a population of 450 neophytes. After secularization, mission property was neglected, the chapel crumbled away, and a ramada made of woven boughs served as a church whenever a priest got out that way.

In 1844 the Santa Ysabel Rancho was granted to José Ortega and his son-in-law, Edward Stokes, and the sorrowful story of Indians being deprived of their lands was repeated. The best part of the valley now belongs to white ranchers, while the Indians are on their reservation where land is stony and soil is poor.

Though for many years the Indians had no adequate chapel, they owned two great and beautiful treasures. Early in the nineteenth century they paid six burro loads of wheat and barley for two mission bells. The bells were laboriously brought from the Rosario Mission in Lower California, and were believed to be the oldest bells in California. One came originally from the Mission of Loreto in Lower California, and bore the inscription "N.S. de Loreto, 1723." The other, dated 1767, was dedicated to San Pedro. San Pedro's bell came from Spain, around the Horn, and while it was being made the Spanish ladies had thrown their gold jewelry into the liquid metal.

At Santa Ysabel two uprights and a cross pole were erected near the roadside, and there the bells hung. An Indian, Enrique La Chusa, rang the bells, and for fifty years he was the official ringer. Despite the fact that one of the bells was cracked, due to the marksmanship of some impious character, they were sweet-toned and pure, and could be heard for miles up and down the valley. Those who remember say that Enrique made a special little melody of the ringing.

On October 13th and 14th, in 1923, there was a great celebration for the bells of Santa Ysabel, for it was their 200th anniversary. Indians came from all the hills and valleys, important dignitaries of the Church came from miles away, and Father Lapointe, who was the missioner in charge, started soliciting funds for a new and beautiful chapel at Santa Ysabel. Eventually his dream came true, and now he is buried beside the wall of the most beautiful Indian chapel in California.

Father Lapointe, well loved by whites and Indians, Catholics and Protestants, served for twenty-nine years as a missionary in San Diego County. He was born in 1875, he died in 1932, and it is said that he preferred to walk, or to ride a horse or mule, over the many trails rather than ever drive a car. Everyone cooperated with Father Lapointe. Indians contributed work and what money they could, ranchers donated money and materials, and in 1924 the chapel was erected.

Then one summer morning, in 1926, the bells were gone. Tracks showed where a light truck had been driven under the cross-pole, but on a paved highway a truck leaves no track.

Enrique must have been heartbroken. Father Lapointe was grieved and mystified. Indians were questioned. Various whites were looked upon with suspicion. Rumors and conjectures flew like winged birds from canyon to canyon, hill to hill. Indians talked among themselves, white people determined to find the bells, a confused legend began to grow. There are now so many stories about the lost bells of Santa Ysabel that a choice can be made of which seems the most interesting.

Each old-timer to whom I talked had his own version of what happened to the bells. One said that the Indians had buried them, waiting for some great event when the bells would be brought forth and rung once more. One said that undoubtedly they had been melted down. (This, I say, could not be. One can't, without being questioned, take two mission bells to a foundry and say, "Here, melt these for me.") Others say the Japanese made ammunition of them, to shoot at Pearl Harbor.

I was told that, until the day he died, Father Lapointe believed that the bells would be restored to their place at Santa Ysabel. But an Indian told me that Father Lapointe knew where the bells were all the time. Another Indian told me that, since the Church owned the bells, it had undoubtedly taken them to some other mission. A third Indian told me he knew who took the bells, but that that person was "dead and gone."

On a day in December, when clouds promised the rain everyone wanted, we went to Santa Ysabel and talked to its young priest, Father Januarius Carillo, who had come here from Italy. Father Carillo, like everyone else, is interested in the story of the bells, had made inquiries, had learned nothing. We had with us an Indian friend, who had been born at Santa Ysabel and baptized by Father Lapointe. When the Indian said the Church surely knew where the bells were, Father Carillo shook his head.

As we went into the chapel a cloud moved away from the sun, and the effect of light on the stained glass windows was purely beautiful. The colors are warm and clear, the workmanship is exquisite. The murals on the walls, done in 1948 by Paul Mathews, are simple, and still so imaginative and rich that one feels how fortunate are the communicants, to be intimate with such beauty.

From the chapel we went to the graveyard, where still there were paper flowers and melted candles left from All Souls Day, when Indian graveyards are alight with tapers. We saw graves of young Indians brought back from overseas battlegrounds, we saw graves of the very old, and graves of young children.

We wandered over the site of the former chapel, saw where the bells had swung and wondered again about the hiding place of the bells of San Pedro and Our Lady of Loreto.

(1950)

The Indians

One of the most unique experiences afforded a visitor to the county is the study of the customs and peculiarities of the Mission Indians, a number of whom have been segregated in government reservations and taught vocational work, and given educational advantages including painting and music. And still the traces of pagan superstition cling to many of them, particularly the old people. And to the student of ethnology, as well as the casual observer, the customs and prejudices of the old "medicine man" days will be unfolded if they are of an observant nature and will take the trouble to investigate these aboriginal surroundings. The primeval fashion of holding fiestas after harvest-time is still followed, but instead of the rude provender which once appeased their appetites at these gatherings—the succulent dried grass-hopper and the toothsome lizard—will be found the ice cream cone, the cheering but not inebriating "pop," and the harmless but necessary peanut. So, too, the fire dance and the war dance have been more or less re-placed by the waltz, the "fox-trot," the "shimmy," and the "bunny hug."

(1921)

The Names That Haunt Me

Russ Leadabrand

With apologies to Stephen Vincent Benét, I have fallen in love with the names on the land in San Diego County. They have always pursued me, noosed me, run along before me and beckoned.

Listen to the hammer-on-anvil tones of Upper Hell-hole and Starvation Mountain and Mother Grundy Peak.

The explorers here who carried the "j's" must have had holes in their knapsacks: they spilled Jamul and Japacha and Japatul and Jacumba in all the delightful places where they rested.

It is a land of animal names, each with the music

of movement: Skunk Spring, Rattlesnake Creek, Fish Creek Wash, Coyote Creek, Chuckwalla Wash, Quail Canyon, Horse Canyon.

And there are places where the place-name parcelers had pure magic in their pens; Wonderstone Wash, Hills of the Moon Wash, Witch Creek, Smuggler Canyon.

There was a time when a man afoot or on horseback could spend a lifetime riding down tree lines and exploring the hidden place-name springs, the mountains of unmapped boulders, the places where meadowlarks call by summer, the canyons that knew old oaks long before the Spanish came and scuffed their acorns.

A man on foot or on horseback could have spent a lifetime building legends, collecting them and running them down.

Were there really jewels to be found in Pala's streambeds? Did gold really shine in the gravels in Coleman Creek? Were there great eagles in those hills overlooking Tecate? Did dinosaurs really leave their footprints at Split Mountain?

And always, for that man on foot or horseback, there would be something in the place-name pouch to call him farther on.

What hid at Hellhole? What was meant by Devil's Punch Bowl? Was there lilac at Lilac? Sage at Sage? Willows at Bow Willow? A grave at Grave Wash?

Today the man afoot is channeled in by macadam and fences, and a man on horseback has an even more difficult chore. But hidden there in the back country of San Diego County there are worded wonders without end for those who would see them. I have looked and I have counted them well. In my notebook I have charted a long list of scenic miracles. True, some are personal, such as a dirt road that runs through a grassy land near Jamul where one day a passing car made a curtain of dust and against that curtain of dust the afternoon sun cast shadows of trees from a distant hill. It was more a thing to sense than to photograph and the wind stirred it quickly and the illusion was gone. But it was a scenic miracle to savor, like the yellow fire that swallows Torrey Pines by spring when the giant coreopsis explode. Yellow fire is uncommon stuff, to be sure, but there was this hillside of it, burning bright, and the smoke that came up was winged: swifts that flew out from the rookeries in the clefted canyons.

To explore the scenic pleasures of San Diego County away from the metropolis, all you need is a reliable map and an inquisitive nature . . . curiosity . . . imagination.

Where does that dirt road lead? The map might offer clues, but it won't tell you of the windrow of eucalyptus you'll find over the hill, standing sentry straight with shaggy bark in the kneedeep grasses. Where does that chaparral tunnel trail lead?

To see San Diego behind the city you need a map and a turn of the curious. If an old house sleeps behind a hedge in the meadowland, stop and look. Check an old windmill at its clanking labors and see if the water that it pushes up from underground is sweet.

Bring your map, and be curious. You can start anywhere. . . .

Always when I'm called to San Diego's back country, with all its charms and mysteries and delights, it's the names on the land that I love most.

Corte Madera and Durasnitos and Mil Piedra. Bell Bluff and Cuyapaipe and Weowlet.

Read the place names and let them gnaw at your curiosity. Let your curiosity lead you here and loose you.

The day of the man afoot or the man on horseback is pretty nearly over. But one thing is sure: You can spend days without number chasing the hawks and swifts and wild pigeons and seabirds in San Diego County's back country and never see it all.

(1969)

VII
When the World Came to San Diego

———— ◆ ————

San Diego may have lost a Republican convention in 1972, but what's a Republican convention compared to one World's Fair in 1915 and another in 1935? The following articles chronicled both the fairs—noting the plans and prospects, the exhibits and attractions, the high hopes and attendant disappointments.

San Diego Ground Breaking

The Carnival and Pageant which San Diego will hold July 19–22 in celebration of the Ground Breaking for the Panama-Pacific Exposition, to be held in the Southern City in 1915, will be made a gala occasion for San Diegans and visitors within its gates. The State will be officially represented, it is announced, in the presence of Governor Johnson and members of his official family. Eloquence and speech-making will occupy a part of the program but the spirit of revelry will brook very little of seriousness and the day will be largely given over to sports and entertainments.

The railroads and steamship companies are making special rates for the occasion and are preparing to handle the multitude of visitors who will travel to this famous California city. Many additional thousands will journey to San Diego by automobile and as the roads en route are in fairly good condition the trip by automobile from the north will be a pleasant one.

This Ground Breaking and Carnival will be the real beginning of San Diego's preparations for the big exposition that they will hold in four years and which San Diego, unaided, will finance and work out into an undoubtedly successful fair. No other city of San Diego's population has ever attempted, without other assistance, such an undertaking as San Diego has in hand for 1915. All of the citizens of San Diego are working for the

141

event with a unanimity of purpose and harmonious accord that has already manifested itself. . . . Every loyal citizen of Southern California—and of all California—will unite with San Diego to make the exposition a credit to the State.

(1911)

Activity at Fairgrounds

It is with a good deal of pride that San Diego is showing visitors progress on the building of the Panama–California Exposition to be held in that city throughout the year 1915. Workmen are busily engaged on the first building, which has just received the roof and is to be completed this spring. It is to be used as the general offices of the exposition company and stands on an eminence in Balboa Park almost in the center of the city of San Diego. From its roof one can see a vista of land and sea fifty miles in all four directions, the purple mountains of Mexico to the south, the Pacific ocean to the west, the Sierras to the east and the coast line to the north. Workmen also are working on the west entrance, where will be built a memorial arch which the Masonic bodies of the state of California will dedicate next April. . . .

One of the most beautiful of the buildings will be the forum, in imitation of ancient Greek and Roman auditoriums. Three sides will be open through which the sound of the concerts and the addresses of noted lecturers will reach thousands of listeners seated on the grass and under trees, the whole shaded and decorated with beautiful and rare trees. A great organ is to be built into this forum; it will be the third building completed, according to present plans.

(1912)

San Diego Beautifies

By January 1, 1915, the date of the opening of the San Diego Exposition, there will not be an unsightly spot in all San Diego. Fences and outhouses are to be overgrown with perennially blooming vines, vacant lots will be cleared and sown with flowers that bloom the year around, houses will be freshly painted, streets cleared of all weeds and rubbish, bare walls adorned with window ledge flower boxes, and hanging baskets from roof ledges, and flower gardens will appear everywhere, until San Diego becomes one great, fragrant, beautiful bouquet. . . .

(1914)

Too Good, Too Gorgeous, Too Magnificent...

If you have not visited the Panama–California Exposition—the San Diego Fair—lose no time but go at once. Make your arrangements, drop everything and go.

True, the Exposition has been opened only a week and it will not close until the night of January 2nd, 1916, but the Fair is too good, too gorgeous, too magnificent to be missed and in delay there is danger. Get ready and go and you will want to stay a long time, for the San Diego Exposition is unique among world's fairs.

San Diego's fair is a new type of exposition and it is as valuable and educational as it is beautiful and its beauty is something which is quite unexampled in exposition history. The fair buildings are uniformly of Spanish architecture whether of mission, cathedral or palace type and the gardens are modeled after the Spanish patios. The plazas and the highways are given Spanish names. The attendants are caballeros and conquistadores and friars and Spanish dancing girls. Two thousand pigeons which nest above the Plaza de Panama alight on the shoulders of the Spanish boys who feed them. It is a scene taken intact from ancient Spain, a breath from the Old World.

A colony of three hundred Indians chosen from the Apaches, Navajos, Supais and other wandering tribes, as well as from the Hopis and Zuñis and other of the pueblo tribes, stalk about the ground and weave their rugs and blankets, shape their pottery and pound out their silver and copper ornaments in the shade of the great adobe pueblos which have been built on a wondrous representation of the Painted Desert of Arizona. And on the Isthmus, which is the great pleasure street of the exposition city, there are the notable features which characterized the old time Pike and Midway and Pay Streak of other expositions. To these have been added some extraordinary novelties and even on this amusement street there is the close attention to accurate details which are necessary to the proper atmosphere, whether it be in the Indian Village or the Hawaiian Village or the streets of Japan or the tunnels of underground Chinatown.

In the same way there has been every attention to the detail in the way of showing the resources of the Southwest. San Diego has established a great citrus orchard within the Exposition grounds where the tourist from the east and the north at any time from January to December can breathe in the exquisite aroma of orange and lemon blossoms and see trees heavy with grapefruit or kumquat or tangerine. He can ramble down the Alameda and see the growing tea plantation, transplanted from Ceylon, the first commercial venture of this sort in the United States. He can wander through the Exhibit Building, along the bridge or along La Via de los Estados and see set before him in convincing array the great resources of the West country. . . .

The man who has covered Europe and Asia and Africa and has neglected his own country will find out that the American West has mountains a little more impressive than the Alps or the Pyrenees or the Himalayas; he will discover that the deserts of the Southwest are a little more appealing than the Sahara and are more wonderfully colored at sunset; he will discover that the antiquities of Greece and Rome and Thebes are not a whit more interesting than those of the red people who centuries ago occupied the western continent—the Aztecs, the Mayas, the Toltecs and the Incas; he will find that the existing tribal life of the Southwest is quite as interesting as the life of the Arab and Hindu and Oriental; he will discover that the fjords of the West are as interesting as those of Scandinavia; he will see forests that are not equaled by any other forests in the world and valleys which are as fertile as any others in the world. In short, at the San Diego Exposition he will see epitomized all the history of the great Southwest. . . .

Three great transcontinental highways now connect the Pacific Coast with the Atlantic Coast and the South and two of these highways have their western terminal in Southern California. Over all of these roadways motor caravans will journey westward during the present year and on each of them roadwork is in progress and sign posting is under way that will expedite the travel of the tourists and aid them in making the long trek with the minimum of discomfort and no confusion concerning the correct route.

Within the state itself roadwork is in progress that will provide California with a notable network of first-class motor roads over which the exposition visitors can travel, before the end of the present year, without ever once leaving a macadam surfaced boulevard. . . .

The officials of the exposition have arranged fully for the reception of their motor guests. The south entrance to the exposition grounds, La Puerta del Sur, and the northern gate, La Puerta del Norte, are retained for automobile admissions. Although no motor cars are permitted within the exposition grounds proper, two large parking spaces, one at the north entrance and the other at the south gate, have been provided which accommodate nearly four hundred automobiles.

In addition to carrying insurance against automobile theft and injury, this exposition concession has made some rather striking innovations. The checkers at the gate, all girls in Spanish costume, furnish the visiting driver a card bearing his license number, retaining in the post-office arrangement a duplicate of that card. The visitor is assisted by attendants garbed in caballero uniform in parking his car where he wishes it and on his return he will have further assistance in getting it out, with opportunity to supply it with gas and oil and secure any minor repairs that are necessary. During his absence the parking space is patrolled regularly and pilfering made impossible, so that rugs, wraps and bundles may be left in the car with safety.

The only vehicle for use within the exposition grounds is a small motor chair known as an "electriquette" which carries two or three people and is limited to a speed of three and one half miles per hour. The speed is easily controlled by the occupants and either passenger can stop the car by stepping on a metal plate in the flooring. There is no chance for it to run away down hill because of the thorough brake system. At the same time it is able to make the easy grades along Calcadas which wind about the brinks of the canyons. Already these little electric "joy-cars" have proved very popular and a constant procession of them make the rounds of the exposition grounds. . . .

That San Diego has a wonderful exposition and one that will more than fulfill the anticipations of the motorist who journeys to it from a distance however great, cannot be emphasized too strongly. It is almost inconceivable that a city with a population of less than seventy-five thousand could have financed and constructed so elaborate and complete an exposition, but that is exactly what San Diego has done and it has opened its fair doors with every debt paid and with money in the treasury.

(1915)

A Plea for Help

The Panama–California Exposition of 1915 has been a failure in no sense of the word. It has been a great success despite the disadvantages under which it was held. But there is a still greater measure of success that is due the enterprise and courage of the citizens of San Diego County. To insure this merited result, a vigorous and systematic campaign has been undertaken throughout Southern California, with the civic associations and the whole citizenship of Los Angeles at its head, to raise funds that will finance the exposition management during the early months of the continuance of the fair.

Everyone is to have the opportunity to help. Everyone is asked to contribute his mite that the eyes of the touring world shall be centered upon Southern California in 1916 and that there may be a world attraction in San Diego that will turn the tide of excursionists into the southern part of the state in volume that will mean prosperity for all of California.

Only a small sum, comparatively, is needed to make certain that the end of 1915 will not witness the closing of San Diego's wonderful fair. Only $75,000 in cash is required to keep open the gates and to preserve, for one year more, an exhibition that is so truly Southern Californian and which so admirably typifies the resources and the beauties and the advantages of this favored portion of the earth. In addition to the small cash fund there is required a guarantee fund in equal amount to be placed at the command of the exposition management in case of need, but which will probably not be touched. . . .

All parts of Southern California are going to profit by the continuation of the Panama–California Exposition. This year the two great fairs that were held in California brought thousands upon thousands of Easterners into California. A large proportion of these tourists visited both the northern and southern parts of the state. Their eyes were opened to the climatic advantages and economic resources of this great commonwealth. They have gone home to talk of the beauties and wonders of California and to advertise it among the very class of people that California desires to attract. Now comes the opportunity to bring them back to us again in 1916. . . .

Let us each one do our small share toward raising the $150,000 cash and guarantee funds that are required.

Let us each do our share toward increasing the success of this all Southern California enterprise by visiting it one or more times during the coming year. Let us each advertise it to our friends in the East in every letter that we write. Let us show our appreciation of the financial courage and public spiritedness of San Diego that made possible the Panama–California Exposition of 1915 and which carried it to success against overwhelming odds. They were a brave people to advance their millions of dollars in the face of strongest competition, unaided by state or government. . . .

Don't delay in mailing your check for one dollar or five dollars or whatever you can afford to send. The funds must be raised without delay. Your help is needed, not in the future, but NOW. The Automobile Club of Southern California has never asked you for aid in any other than matters of purely personal interest to motorists. Here is something for the good of all Southern California. Address your letter to. . . .

(1915)

A New Fair for San Diego
Raúl Rodriguez

Why?

Why do cities have world fairs?

Why should San Diego?—and why at this particular time?

The California–Pacific International Exposition is a precedent-smasher all the way through, beginning with the events that gave birth to the idea and the fantastic chain of circumstances that made the show possible.

Most world fairs are staged with an eye to the past. They are observances of past events like the completion of the Panama Canal, or commemorations of closed epochs, like Philadelphia's Sesquicentennial or Chicago's Century of Progress.

San Diego's exposition is strictly a thing of the future. The year 1935 marks not the end but the beginning of an epoch in the West. Colossal works like Boulder Dam, the Colorado River Aqueduct, the All-American Canal, and Grand Coulee Dam are creating wealth so great that it taxes one's imagination just to think about it—wealth to be enjoyed not by past or present generations, but by those yet unborn.

The California–Pacific exposition is a gesture of hope in the future rather than pride in the past.

But why in San Diego?

Only because San Diego has unsurpassed facilities for the exposition, and because her businessmen were the first to muster up enough courage to put it on. For the exposition really belongs not only to San Diego and California, but to all the West. . . .

To tell the story from the beginning, we have to go back twenty years to the Panama–California Exposition, San Diego's last big show. To house this fair, San Diegans built in Balboa Park a group of buildings and gardens so exquisitely beautiful that the park soon became the most famous spot in San Diego, and one of California's proudest possessions.

The exposition over, a few of the permanent buildings were put into service as museums, libraries, administration units. The rest, emptied, began to fall prey to the elements and the termites. Meanwhile, the beauty of Balboa Park and its palaces was loudly and justly praised by every California booster, and Balboa Park became a symbol, an epitome of San Diego's loveliness.

Then suddenly one day about three years ago, a palm tree in San Diego's plaza fell over, killing a little girl. Investigation showed that the palm had been completely eaten out by termites; and San Diego's new city manager, scared by visions of similar tragedies to come, ordered investigations of all questionable structures in San Diego.

The fire chief, police chief, building inspector, health officer and city electrician went to work, and in due time they got around to the buildings in Balboa Park.

The five officials reported that the palaces were hopelessly dangerous, that all should be razed immediately and the ground landscaped. There was also a project favored by some councilmen to build a mammoth civic auditorium on the ground hallowed by Goodhue's masterpieces.

When these recommendations became known, San Diegans generally were up in arms. To raze the buildings that meant so much to San Diego was bad enough, but to sully the ground with a "colossal" auditorium was downright sacrilege. The chamber of commerce protested vehemently, and formed its own citizens' committee to determine independently whether the buildings were really in such bad shape.

One of the committee members was Richard S. Requa, a veteran architect who possessed considerable ability and a blunt manner of stating his convictions. He found that it was not only quite feasible to restore the buildings, but that it would actually cost less to do it than to raze them and landscape the ground. . . .

In its setting, the California–Pacific International Exposition is as different from traditional world fairs as it was in its origin and growth. Balboa Park was not created or remodeled especially for the exposition. It has been there as long as California itself, and for more than twenty years its gardens and landscapes have been care-fully developed, with a constant striving for true, per-manent beauty. . . .

One part of the exposition will be entirely Spanish Renaissance—buildings, gardens, decoration, all will follow the strictest traditions of medieval Spain. Here you will see the Palace of Foods and Beverages, of Parent and Child, of Fine Arts, the House of Hospitality, the Museum of Natural History, and other exhibits of like nature.

The Industrial Mesa, completely out of sight of the Renaissance palaces, will be occupied by buildings of a more modern trend—exhibits of oil companies, manu-facturers and such. . . .

In the design of some of the modern buildings, Lar-rinaga and Requa have developed a striking new style which will undoubtedly prove one of the most interest-ing things about the exposition.

They borrowed from the Pueblo Indians their use of broad, low wall areas, which gives the buildings a racy, modern flavor. They broke up the monotony of these blank spaces by adding a few—a very few—bands of ornamental design lifted bodily from the Aztec and Maya. Then they built into the cornices, as integral parts of the buildings, huge planting-boxes from which living flowers will trail down, making live decoration for the inanimate walls. The result is an entirely new style, thoroughly modern, based solidly on good Western traditions and exactly fitted to California's natural con-ditions.

Still another separate area will be turned over to the Midway, the hey-hey department of the exposition. Here architecture has been thrown to the winds. Such things as midget villages, freak animals, two-headed baby shows, the flea circus and their like just can't be con-fined within architectural traditions. Architect Requa himself admits that when the Midway came up for consideration, he threw up his hands and forgot it.

Down in one of the deep, twisting canyons will be an exhibit that could have a place only in a California exposition—Golden Gulch. Golden Gulch is an exact reproduction of a 'forty-nine mining camp, complete with general store, saloon, Chinese laundry and restaurant, iron-barred bank and sheriff's office, etc. Up on the hill a model mine will be set up, and down in the river-bottom prospectors will do a little placer mining. The only way to reach Golden Gulch will be by stagecoach or burroback, and once there you'll feel as if you were really in an old mine camp, for all the rest of the world will be invisible above the steep canyon sides.

There will be authentic Taos and Zuñi pueblos where real live Indians will practice their arts and crafts. The Women's Palace will also be traditionally Indian in style. Here milady will get her fill of fashions, beauty aids and so forth. . . .

The exposition will succeed without a doubt. Even if one could remain unconvinced by the matchless setting and the swarming construction going on in the grounds, a few minutes' talk with some of the exposition workers would make a booster out of him.

Failure just isn't possible when people are willing to work so hard to put a thing over—especially when they seem to be having so much fun doing it.

(1935)

VIII
Famous (and Not So Famous) San Diego Firsts

During the Depression, Touring Topics ran a contest called "Famous California Firsts." Readers could earn $1 for each "famous first" deemed by the editors to be worthy of publication. San Diego came in for its fair share of firsts, as the next few pages will attest. The results were published in January, 1933.

First elopement in California was that of Josefa Carillo and Henry Delano Fitch, assisted by Pío Pico, the bride's cousin. They left San Diego on the *Vulture,* in 1828, and were married at Valparaiso, Chile. It caused a tremendous sensation and an ecclesiastical trial of the culprits at San Gabriel.

First excommunication uttered against a member of the Roman Catholic faith in California was pronounced at Mission San Diego in 1775 when Fernando Rivera y Moncada, a military commandant of California, demanded custody of an Indian neophyte who had sought sanctuary in the improvised chapel after being accused of complicity in the killing of Fray Luís Jaume and other Spaniards during a revolt. On refusal of the priests to surrender the Indian, Rivera, sword in hand, entered the chapel and removed the suspect, whereupon Fray Juan Fuster, guardian of the mission, launched at him the anathema of excommunication.

First vaccinations made in California were done by James Ohio Pattie, an American trapper and "sometimes surgeon extraordinary to his Excellency, the Governor of California." He went from mission to mission, started from San Diego, and in less than four months had vaccinated 22,000 persons, the entire population of Alta, California, completing his task in January, 1829.

First Christian religious services, consisting of a Catholic mass, were conducted November 12, 1602, on the shores of San Diego Bay by Carmelite friars attached to the exploration expedition of Sebastián Vizcaíno.

First permanent settlement in California was started when soldiers and sailors of the "holy expedition" of 1769, under the command of Vicente Vila, Fernando Javier Rivera y Moncada, and Pedro Fages, on May 17, 1769, were moved from a temporary camp on San Diego Bay, to North or Old Town, at the foot of Presidio Hill.

First hot springs to be discovered and recorded were Warner Hot Springs in San Diego County, found by Father Juan Mariner of San Diego Mission, in 1795. The springs at present discharge 200,000 gallons of water daily, at a uniform temperature of 140° Fahrenheit.

First earthquake recorded in California by Spaniards was experienced by Gaspar de Portolá, on his first journey from San Diego in search of Monterey.

First public execution took place at San Diego, April 11, 1778, when Sergeant José Francisco Ortega ordered four Diegueño Indian chiefs shot for rebellion.

First martyr was Father Luís Jayme, who was slain by Indians at San Diego Mission, November 4, 1775, during the course of an attack and the burning of the establishment by the aborigines.

First extended account of California printed in the United States, was that written by Captain William Shaler of the *Lelia Bird,* and published in the *American*

Register in 1808, under the title *Journal of a Voyage Between China and the Northwestern Coast of America, Made in 1804.*

First raising of American flag on California soil took place at San Diego early 1829. Captain James P. Arthur who, with a small party, had been sent ashore from the *Brookline* to cure hides, erected a small barn as a storehouse and for living quarters. Life was lonely, and to attract passing ships the sailors made an American flag from the vari-colored shirts of the party, and raised it over the barn whenever a sail was sighted. The flag was not intended to denote American sovereignty. Later the same flag is said to have been raised many times at Santa Barbara.

First electric telegraph in California dates from September 22, 1853, when the opening of the line from Point Lobos Lighthouse to the Merchant's Exchange, San Francisco, a total distance of eight miles, was celebrated in a manner befitting so important an event.

First mission was founded in Alta, California, by Junípero Serra on July 16, 1769, at San Diego.

First irrigation project in California was undertaken and completed by the padres of Misión San Diego. It consisted of a stone dam 254 feet long, 12 feet thick and 14 feet high, and a 12-mile stone-and-tile flume from the site of the dam in Mission Gorge to the mission lands. It was completed early in 1781 and portions of the dam and aqueduct still remain.

First county to be created in California was San Diego County following the Constitutional Convention in

Monterey in 1849. Early the next year the American State of California became a reality.

First white child born in California was Salvador Ygnacio Linares, son of Ygnacio and Gertrudis Rivas Linares, of the overland expedition of Juan Bautista de Anza from Sonora to California. The birth took place at Middle Willows, near the Arroyo Santa Catarina, which is in the vicinity of Warner's Hot Springs, December 24, 1775.

First Indian hostilities with the Spanish in California took place at San Diego, September 28, 1542. That night some of Cabrillo's men went ashore to fish with a net and three of them were wounded by arrows shot by some nearby Indians.

First church bells were brought to San Diego aboard the *San Carlos* or *San Antonio* in 1769. Until recently they hung in the belfry of the Church of the Immaculate Conception at Old Town, San Diego.

First organ mentioned in California history was a barrel organ presented to the then father-president of the missions, Fermín de Lasuén, by Captain George Vancouver, while they were both at San Diego in December, 1793. The contraption was taken to Misión San Carlos. It is now in the museum at Misión San Juan Bautista and bears the maker's inscription: "Dobbs, 22 Swan St., London."

First bishop of California was Francisco García Diego y Moreno, who arrived at San Diego from Mexico, December 11, 1841, and proceeded thence to Misión Santa Bárbara, which he made his seat. He administered the sacrament of confirmation the first time in his diocese to 125 persons in the presidio chapel at San Diego.

First open-air Greek theater in California was constructed in 1901 by Mrs. Katherine Tingley of Theosophical Society, located on Point Loma.

First reinforced concrete viaduct of cantilever unit type ever built in California, is the Cabrillo Bridge, located in Balboa Park, San Diego.

First "naval" encounter between an American vessel and a Spanish fort in Upper California waters took place at San Diego between the American ship *Lelia Byrd* and the guns at Fort Guijarros, on March 22, 1803.

IX
Depression Dining
Sharon Thoreau

———◆———

Since the 1930s the *Westways* restaurant column has been among the most popular of the magazine's regular features. Most of the San Diego dining establishments listed here are long vanished, but a few still exist. However, times have changed. Please don't walk into the elegant Hotel Del Coronado and ask for the $2 dinner you read about in *San Diego and the Back Country*. You'll probably be thrown out—elegantly, of course.

The Golden Lion Tavern

It is one of the oldest eating places in the city, having been there for twenty-five years. It is also an attractive one, with a gabled brick front suggestive of an old English tavern. Mounted game trophies and English sporting prints decorated the walls, dominated by a huge golden lion. The food, however, is not designed, as you might suspect, entirely for the hearty men of the open. There is a staggering variety, to be sure, but many of them lean to the epicurean side. Frog legs with bacon, for instance; and broiled jumbo squab on toast. From the soup tureen you may select green turtle soup or French onion. Desserts give you, as the best choice, apple strudel with lemon sauce. Wines and beers; no music or dancing. Open 7 A.M. to 2 A.M. *(1935)*

Rosso's Tavern

Unless you are in the know, you might pass Rosso's Tavern at Pacific Beach without noticing it. You'll know it by the horde of cars parked outside, unless you're lucky enough to get there early, in which case you'll perhaps get a table without having to wait for it. Rosso's is popular in those parts, and for good cause: the cause including roast pork as you never ate before, homemade pastries, and coffee fit for gods or mortals. Special plate dinner, 75¢; other meals, 35-50¢. Service in coffee shop or dining-room. No liquors, and no music or dancing. *(1935)*

Torrey Pines Lodge

Three guesses as to the best way of reaching Torrey Pines Lodge! There's the old Torrey Pines road that veers off from Highway 101 at the foot of the new grade; or there's a short trek back from the top of the new road. And finally there's a spot on the new road where you can park the car and hike up over the cliffs to the glorious site of Torrey Pines Park and its Indian lodge. For one who has had luncheon not too long before, I recommend the third method of approach. By the time you get there you'll be ready for luncheon, dinner or afternoon tea, as the case may be. Our case was tea, with hot cinnamon toast and marmalade, and small cakes, served on a sheltered sunny terrace. Luncheon and dinner from noon to 8 P.M. with prices from 50¢ to 75¢. Fried chicken is a specialty here, too. No liquors served. *(1935)*

Fulton's Lone Tree

Nearly thirty years ago, Anna Held built a rambling, many-windowed home on the cliffs overlooking La Jolla caves. Made of California redwood, it had a friendly German touch in the inscriptions carved into hearth and doorway panels. And these hospitable greetings are just as appropriate today, when the house is known as Fulton's Lone Tree, at the Sign of the Green Dragon. The Fultons specialize in hospitality and friendly atmosphere. Incidentally, they specialize in food that's a bit different. From twenty-five years' residence in the Orient, they have brought back exotic Eastern recipes which they are gradually introducing to their patrons. Try some of the curried meats; or Russian borscht soup. That doesn't mean, however, that more familiar dishes are not included. Fried chicken is a superior brand, as I can testify; and the cakes all have a homemade touch. Entertainment on Sunday nights by Spanish troubadours. Luncheons, teas, dinners, 50¢ to $1. *(1935)*

The Twin Roosters

If you can whiz by those roosters outside the big, old-fashioned white house at the southern end of Carlsbad you'll have more power of food-resistance than I had. The Twin Inns, they call it, but it will go down in California history as the Twin Roosters, even though there are three sets of them. It's a landmark, that old inn, built as a private home in 1887, and famous since 1919 for superlative fried chicken, smoking hot and seasoned with an artist's hand. There is no a la carte service here; merely your choice of chicken or steak, with just enough trimmings to make up a meal worth eating. The dining room is large, with dance floor and bar; however dances are confined to private parties arranged for in advance. "Open from 11 A.M. to ?" the sign at the entrance reads; and this I found, is true. So long as guests arrive, just that long they will be served. Luncheon, $1.00, dinner, $1.50; special prices for children. Liquors served. *(1935)*

Hotel Del Coronado

The Hotel del Coronado is one of the oldest and finest hostelries in the West, and ranks among the nation's best. It is a citadel of peace, urbane good manners, and refinement. It is no place to snatch a hasty snack, but one cannot imagine a more pleasant place to spend a couple of hours over a meal or a few days of perfect relaxation. The service, of course, is impeccable. The exterior of the hotel, its rambling wooden pavilions, its tiny peaked towers bristling with dormers, its multitude of windows, is a masterpiece of nineteenth-century building. The interior has been modernized for comfort, but enough of the Victorian has been retained to make a visit thoroughly delightful. The bar has not been changed one whit since building, and it is a masterpiece of carved mahogany and brass. In the dining room, table d'hôte breakfast is served from 7 to 9, at $1; luncheon from 12:30 to 2 at $1.55; dinner from 6:30 to 8 at $2. There is no music or dancing in the dining room, but dances are held in the Ocean Terrace Room daily except Monday, in the Circus Casino Saturdays, and in the Crown Room at dinner on Thursdays. A grill adjoins the bar, serving snacks and specialties. Wines and liquors are served throughout the hotel. *(1940)*

Saddlerock Grill and Lounge, *1126 Fourth Avenue, San Diego*

This is one of the fine restaurants which have made San Diego a pleasant place to be in at mealtime. Tastefully decorated in sound, restful modern style, the dining room reflects the high quality of the food offered. Such specialties as lobster thermidor, charcoal-broiled club sirloin and hangtown fry highlight a menu of widely varied à la carte specialties. Table d'hôte prices are as follows: Breakfast, 25 to 50 cents; luncheon 25 cents and up; dinner from 60 cents to $1.25. The restaurant is open from 7 A.M. until midnight, the bar next door opening about mid-morning. No music nor dancing. Liquors and wines are served. *(1940)*

The U.S. Grant Hotel

Boasts an excellent coffee shop, a rendezvous specializing in quick-order specialties and a cocktail lounge. Service and quality in all these rooms is eminently good, as befits one of San Diego's leading commercial hotels. The Coffee Shop is open from 6:30 A.M. to 9 P.M.,

serving a wide choice of à la carte specialties, and table
d'hôte meals. Breakfast prices go from 25 to 50 cents;
luncheon 55 cents and some specialties at other prices;
dinner $1. Liquor is served from the bar. There is no
music or dancing. The rendezvous serves quick orders
from 11 A.M. to 2 P.M and special dinners from 5 P.M.,
pricing ranging from 45 cents to $1. The cocktail lounge
downstairs is open daily from 4 P.M. to 1 A.M., closed
Sundays. On the Sabbath you can get dinner at the
rendezvous from noon on. The U.S. Grant is, in fine, one
of the leading hostelries of the Pacific Coast and you
may enter its dining rooms perfectly confident of being
well served. *(1940)*

Friedhof's Diner, *Pacific Boulevard (Highway No. 101)*
and Laurel, San Diego
The idea of setting up a restaurant in a railroad car,
or reasonable facsimile, is an old one, but Friedhof's
Diner is the modern expression of the old idea. The
cars are streamlined, aluminum-painted, ultra-modern,
coupled into a two-car unit, one unit being a first-class
dining room, the other a tourist-class coffee shop. The
food and service in both cars is first-class. Featured is
the charcoal broiler whence come succulent Omaha
steaks and a specially prepared super-hamburger, made
of ground sirloin. Fish, fowl and other specialties are
also served. Wines and beer (but no liquor) are
served. No music or dancing. Table d'hôte luncheons are
40 to 60 cents, dinners 75 cents to $1.35. Steak spe-
cials are from 50 cents for the super-hamburger to
$1.15 for a New York cut. Hot biscuits after 5 P.M.
(1940)

Emerald Hills Country Club, *Broadway Extension*
about 6 miles east of Fifth and Broadway, San Diego
One of San Diego's most favored suburban night

spots. A first-rate orchestra plays for dancers every evening, including Sunday, until 2 A.M. and the gaiety is heightened by two floorshows every night. The Club, however, is open from 9 in the morning and is well patronized for breakfast and luncheon by San Diegans who arise early to enjoy golf, riding, trap-shooting and skeet-shooting on the Club grounds. Table d'hôte breakfasts are 50 cents, luncheon 65 cents to $1.25, dinner $1.25 to $2.50. No cover charge. All wines and liquors are served. Banquet rooms are available for parties. The club, though gay, is quite orderly and extremely well conducted. *(1940)*

El Cordova Cafe and Coffee Shop, *1351 Orange Avenue, Coronado*

Tasteful and airily done in modified Spanish colonial style, the Cordova hotel is an ornament to a community already distinguished for its pleasing architectural aspect. The interior of the Cordova coffee shop is in keeping with its welcoming outside aspect. Charcoal–broiled steaks, fowl, seafood and other specialties are served in the dining room, and wines and liquors from the Rose Bowl, connecting bar. The coffee shop is open from 7 A.M to 9 P.M. The à la carte selection is wide, and includes malted milks and milkshakes but no other fountain specialties. Table d'hôte breakfasts are from 25 to 50 cents, lunches 35 and 40 cents, dinner from 65 cents to $1.25 *(1940)*

Deauville Cafe, *Third Ave. at the Plaza*

Formerly Howard's; now modern in decor. Highly regarded by such natives as appreciate dining, dancing and a floor show. Prices: $1.25 to $2. Liquor served; no couvert or minimum. *(1932)*

San Diego Hotel Coffee Room, *339 Broadway, San Diego*

The San Diego hotel, one of the city's leading downtown hostelries, prides itself on its coffee room. The room itself is spacious and cheery, and its neighboring bar is snugly gay. Coffee room specialty is a sizzling steak at $1. Its à la carte selection is varied but not too bewilderingly wide. Table d'hôte breakfasts are 25 to 50 cents; luncheons 60 and 65 cents, the 60-cent item being a generous businessman's lunch; dinners are from 75 cents to $1.25. The coffee room is open from 6:30 A.M. to 9 P.M., the bar from 10 A.M. to 2 A.M. All wines and liquors are served in the coffee room as well as in the bar and cocktail lounge. There is no music or dancing. *(1940)*

Bernardini's, *2110 Belt St.*

Noble Italian cookery and excellent seafood. Prices: 50 cents to $1.15 (10 cents extra for toasted Italian bread, and worth it). Hours 11 A.M. to 9 P.M. Closed Mondays except holidays. Wines and beer served; no music; no couvert. *(1938)*

Chevrier's Grill, *Solana Beach*

There is no finer food served anywhere on the Coast Highway, big cities included, than the faultless fare at Chevrier's. The chef, Georges Payan, presided for many years over the kitchen of the California Club in Los Angeles, and it is a treat for the general public to be able to enjoy his masterpieces at the modest prices he charges. The cuisine is French, of the very highest order. Every dish that comes out of the kitchen is seasoned to a king's taste. Outstanding are salads, grilled mushrooms on toast with Canadian bacon, seafood au gratin. Chevrier's is no place to dash in for a quick snack. You should take your time over such food. Wines and beer—Beaulieu wines are served, but no hard liquor. There is no music or dancing. Lunch is 55 cents, dinner $1, $1.25 and $1.50. *(1940)*

La Valencia Hotel, *1132 Prospect Ave., La Jolla*
Hungry or not, you'll always stop at beautiful La Jolla to explore the cliffs and the caves. And in case you strike it at mealtime, better jot down the name of La Valencia Hotel. Easy of access from the highway, and plainly marked, this colorful Spanish hostelry has a small, attractive café that looks out on the front courtyard, and is bright with sunshine and amber glass. Food is real food here, too, and well served. Excellent steaks and chops. Meals are served only during meal hours, with prices from 65¢ to $1 for luncheon and dinner. *(1935)*

The Brass Rail, *530 "B" St., San Diego*
The fun of going to The Brass Rail lies in jumping down from your stool at the counter and helping yourself from the center buffet, where you can see salads, sandwiches and other snacks made up while you wait. You may, if you're uppish, lounge at tables in the adjoining room, and demand service; but you'll most likely do as the others do, and serve yourself. Drop in late at night: midnight appetizers are a special pride and joy of this establishment. There's a special Virginia "hickory sugar-cured" ham on rye sandwich, and a special seafood cocktail bar; both of them, worth sampling. All the cocktails are not seafood, however. The Brass Rail offers a long list of liquors. Full luncheons and dinners include all kinds of charcoal-broiled meats and game, with the spotlight on chicken and squab, sautéed in wine, not to mention baked potatoes, hot biscuits and honey. They're modestly proud, too, of a special chicken patty à la King. And if you should fancy a golden buck, or

a nice Scotch woodcock, or boneless pigs-feet with vinaigrette sauce, they are yours. Desserts, you will find, are soft pedaled. Open from 11 A.M. to 2 A.M. Dinner, 65¢ to $1. *(1935)*

Heidelberg Tavern, *1058 Fifth Avenue, San Diego*
Step over to the next street, descend a flight of steps into a softly-lighted basement, and you will be in Heidelberg Tavern, one of San Diego's popular eating and dancing spots. From the name and from its appearance you will expect to hear steins banged on the table and good songs ringing clear at any moment. In this, however, you'll be disappointed. There is a bar and a dance floor, but revelry is restrained. San Diego people go to the Heidelberg for good food as well as for a good time. Dinners, priced from 50¢ to 85¢, offer an alluring filet mignon, and calves sweetbreads sauté, among other good things. After-theater service is à la carte, with such characteristic delicacies as Weiner schnitzel, German pancakes, and spaghetti with sweetbreads. Open from 11 A.M. Liquors, music and dancing. *(1935)*

Vincent's Dining Room, *2720 Fourth Avenue, San Diego*
One of a number of family-style homecooking restaurants established in fine old homes in the better residential sections of San Diego. Vincent's occupies a grand three-story brick mansion protected from prying eyes by a high brick wall. By throwing together the living room, dining room, library and other rooms, it has achieved a large, yet cozy single dining hall. The cooking is American home style, and the clientele consists of sound, respectable home citizens. No wines or liquors are served, and there is no music or dancing. Open daily from 11:30 A.M. to 2 P.M. for lunch (50¢ to $1); from 4:30 P.M. to 8 P.M. for dinner (same prices). Sunday

hours are continuous from 11:30 A.M. to 8 P. M. Vincent's entertains a vast number of luncheon parties and bridge luncheons in the private dining-rooms upstairs. *(1940)*

The Savoy, *1055 Fourth Avenue, San Diego*
Almost next door to this tavern is The Savoy, recently renovated, and shining with new coats of paint. It is a quiet place, centrally located, with deft and pleasant service. Seafood is a specialty here, prepared by a cosmopolitan chef who has cooked his way around the world. You will find epicurean frogs legs here, too, as well as more plebeian fare. Lunches 30¢ to 50¢; dinners to $1. Liquors; no music or dancing. *(1935)*

Mrs. Malleson's, *716 Second Street, Oceanside*
Home cooking, American family style, and extremely popular with Oceanside residents. The restaurant occupies a huge old mansion some three blocks off the main highway, and Mrs. Malleson offers substantial luncheons and dinners, both 65 cents table d'hôte. The menu usually includes a choice of four meats; vegetables are all fresh and carefully chosen. Mrs. Malleson particularly prides herself on her scalloped eggplant. Luncheon hour is from 11:30 A.M. to 1:30 P.M., dinner from 5:30 to 7:30 P.M. No wines or liquors are served, and there is no music or dancing. *(1940)*

El Cortez, *Seventh Avenue and Ash St.*
Quiet dining in the elegant tradition in one of San Diego's newest hotels. Prices: moderate. Liquor served; no music; no couvert. *(1938)*

Pastore's, *8th Avenue and Broadway;*
Caesar's, *6th Avenue and University, San Diego*
Two brothers and their brother-in-law operate the

twin cafés, Pastore's and Caesar's; and the cooking must be a family affair, since the same things are served at both places, and the same menu cards used. You will go to either place for the kind of ravioli and spaghetti you have always dreamed about but never tasted; served in heaping, steaming platefuls with mushroom sauce and grated Parmesan cheese. A half-and-half order, combining the two dishes, or serving tagliarini with either one, is a wise choice. Antipasto, salami and other Italian appetizers are on the list, and, according to the menu card, "only the best" wines are served. Full dinners, 75¢; including steak, chicken, or ham, with Italian dishes on the side. Ravioli or spaghetti, 35¢. No music or dancing. Wines, beers, and mixed drinks. Open 11 A.M. to 9 P.M. *(1935)*

Foreign Club, *Tijuana*
When in Mexico, do as the Americans do, and eat at the Foreign Club in Tijuana. It isn't Mexican, to be sure, this big, luxurious dining room done in clever modern manner; but there is Mexican service and cookery, and Mexican entertainment during the floor show; and the best capons south or north of the border. Also such tidbits as swordfish steak sauté with walnut butter and bacon; and seafood à la Newburg with au gratin border of rice. Jot down on your cuff, too, that you mustn't pass up the banana fritters, nor broiled tomatoes. They know what to do with them there. Wine or beer served with meals; also an impressive à la carte list. Dancing and music during meal hours. Floor shows at 2:30 and 8 P.M. Luncheon, 60¢, dinner, $1.00. *(1935)*

Carlsbad Hotel, *Highway 101, Carlsbad*
The hotel, a rambling Spanish colonial building, is a landmark on the coast highway between San Diego and Los Angeles. Both the coffee shop and the dining room

are open to the public, serving food of a standard in keeping with the hotel service, which is of a high order. Hours are from 7 A.M. to 10 P.M. daily; 8A.M. to 10 P.M. Sunday. A wide choice of à la carte breakfast dishes appears on the menu, plus a number of club breakfasts at 35 to 60 cents. Lunches are 45, 55, and 65 cents; dinner from 85 cents to $1, with a special steak dinner at 95 cents. The coffee shop is spacious and comfortable, and there is a snug bar in connection. Guests enjoy dancing to phonograph music. *(1940)*

Café Del Rey Moro, *Balboa Park*
The Exposition's House of Hospitality successfully perpetuated as a first-class restaurant. Specialties: Tea (2 to 5 P.M.), and al fresco dining. Prices: Luncheon, 55 cents to $1; steak dinner for two, $1.85. No liquor served; no music; no couvert. *(1938)*

The Red Apple Inn, *Carlsbad-by-the-Sea*
Ever since the day we used to polish them lovingly and lay them on teacher's desk, red apples have stood for something extra nice. So when the proprietors of San Luis Rey Inn, that hospitable inn at the northern end of Carlsbad-by-the-Sea, changed its name to the Red Apple, they chose something that struck the popular fancy. Red apples decorate the highway sign, and the menu cards, and get your mouth all fixed for something special in the way of food even before it's served. You won't be disappointed. The New York steak is something to write home about; and you won't forget breaded pork chops as they serve them there, either. Strange as it may seem, the thing that stands out most is superlative tapioca pudding, creamy, flavorsome and not just another tapioca pudding.

There is charm and leisurely comfort at this country inn, with personal, friendly service. The only improvement I suggest is a barrel of red apples in the lobby, for souvenirs. Luncheon and dinner, 75¢, $1.00. Beer served. No music or dancing. *(1935)*

Paul's Inn, *1245 Fourth Ave.*
One of San Diego's two best night spots. Dinner only (6 P.M. to 2 A.M.). Prices: $1 to $2. Liquor served. Music, dancing and entertainment. No couvert or minimum. *(1938)*

George's, *Cardiff*
Since 1915, George's has been a place where they serve better lobster than in any other spot known to epicures. At least, so I've been told, and after one of George's lobster dinners, I'll swear to its truth. It is an unpretentious white frame building along the beach at Cardiff; but it has a reputation—*and* it has lobster. They serve it steamed and gently removed from the shell in a perfect pink crescent, with a delicate green crown of peas. And with the first bite, you'll learn just how good unbelievably good lobster can be. A full dinner goes with it, of course, for $1.25. There are steaks and other goods, incidentally, for the same price. Open all day, with full meals served from noon on. *(1935)*

X
Notes from "Tides West"

Carey McWilliams

————◆————

For many years Carey McWilliams wrote the column "Tides West" in *Westways*. The following selections from those columns may give us a taste of his incisive, often humorous view of the foibles and follies of the times.

The Hollywood Theater in San Diego, on a sultry August evening, offered its distinguished patrons a mild midsummer night's entertainment: *The French Nudist,* "the only authentic and uncensored picture ever filmed in an actual nudist colony," with, as an added and wholly irresistible attraction, *The Killing of Clyde Barrow and Bonnie Parker* which ". . . shows some of the highlights in the lives of these daring criminal sweethearts from Texas, including the scenes of the actual killing. The spectator is given the opportunity to see these sweethearts of gangland as they lay in their bullet-riddled car." *(1934)*

During the month of October, "the notorious southwestern outlaw," Charles "Pretty Boy" Floyd, was seen miraculously throughout the state. He was observed in Santa Barbara, "by a man who knows him"; when seen he was "driving west in a dark sedan." The ubiquitous Floyd later was seen in Los Angeles, "on his way to San Francisco." (Just how his destination was ascertained was not revealed.) In Ventura he was seen by "a man who knew him in Oklahoma." He appeared in Oakland, Fresno, and San Francisco, and was last seen speeding through San Diego, "by a man who knew him well." *(1933)*

The residents of Kensington Heights, San Diego, organized an "old-fashioned hair-cutting club—no membership dues, or passwords—just a neighborly spirit and a head of hair that needs attention." *(1933)*

While in San Diego, the True Vow Keepers Club, comprised of 194 couples who have married for fifty years or more, had a picnic lunch at Ramona's Marriage Place. Gingerbread with whipped cream was served with punch. *(1933)*

Of the numerous indigenous social forums created in California none is more respected or admired than the True Vow Keepers Clubs which thrive throughout the state. San Diego has a large and flourishing unit of these "long-time married couples," which periodically convenes to indulge, with public immodesty, a sense of the virtue of longevity. At a recent meeting, a local pastor delivered a discourse on *How to Approach the End of the Journey* in a church that had been specially decorated for the meeting as "an old-fashioned living room —the family Bible and album on the center table, and other homey features that carried the elderly couples back to early days when they were newlyweds." The public is always welcome to these meetings where the true vow keepers occupy chairs near the pulpit, seated in the order of their seniority in servitude. *(1935)*

One of the few authentic folk heros in modern California is Charles Hatfield, the rain-maker. Hatfield is the California Paul Bunyan. Tall tales will be bold in the future of his achievements—tales considerably taller than his achievements which, in themselves, are remarkable enough. He was greeted in Oakland, on his honeymoon, by a "fairly heavy drizzle of rain," which he promptly disclaimed. Hatfield is not the man to acknowledge paternity of a drizzle: when he disturbs the elements, *it rains.*

Mr. Hatfield gave an interesting interview to the press. He first began to experiment with "the possibilities of rain making back in 1903 and 1904," when Southern California was suffering from a condition which, after the lapse of all these years, may now safely be referred to as a "drought." Since then he has "not had a single failure in more than thirty public rain-making contracts," the last of which was in Honduras in 1930.

Perhaps the most remarkable Hatfield achievement was in San Diego in 1916 when, within a period of twenty-six days after his equipment had been set up, he filled the 18,000,000,000-gallon reservoir with water —"a phenomenon that has never been repeated," as he modestly explains. On another occasion, in the Mojave Desert near Randsburg, he produced forty inches of rain in three hours, the heaviest rain ever recorded in the United States.

And who will gainsay the miracle-working providence of one who can even imagine rain at Randsburg? The most fascinating part of the Hatfield history is the secrecy with which the process is guarded. No one, he says, has ever succeeded in discovering his methods of attracting rain or in duplicating his remarkable feats; he has kept his process carefully guarded. "I do not doubt," he remarks, "that my method would have saved all the tremendous losses of the dust bowl, had it been called into play." It is not by accident that the major hero of a desert region should be a rain-maker. And Hatfield is a folk hero: he rightfully belongs in the company of Riley, Bunyan, and Pecos Bill. *(1937)*

In San Diego, a local bard has composed a very popular song, *"My Sunshine."* It is sung to the tune of *"O Sole Mio."* I quote:

Oh, Escondido,
Encinitas, Pala,
Jacumba, Mesa Grande,
Tijuana
Oh, Coronado,
El Cajón, Dulzura,
La Jolla, Chula Vista,
Cuyamaca.

CHORUS:
Oh, San Diego,
Santee, Del Mar,
Las Flores, Poway,
Oh, Palomar
Jamul,
Encanto, Otay
San Luis Rey,
San Onofre.

(1933)

Edmund Wilson has returned from Europe and once again the eastern reviews are carrying his brilliant criticism, and, once again, the fur is flying, for Wilson, like John Jay Chapman whose work he greatly admires, delights in speaking his mind.

Prior to the death of his wife, victim of a strange accident (she slipped, on entering the Paseo courtyard in Santa Barbara, and struck the base of her skull on the curbing), Wilson occasionally visited in California. He was in Los Angeles in the fall of 1931, studying California curiosa, as readers of three lively chapters in *The American Jitters* have discovered. It was a pleasure, at that time, to introduce Mr. Wilson to such interesting personalities as Mrs. Aimee McPherson, Dr. Gustave Briegleb, Dave Clark, and the Reverend Robert Shuler, all of whom are unforgettably limned in the uncannily observant prose that Wilson employs to record his sociological impressions.

Later, on the occasion of this same visit, I drove Wilson to San Diego, where we investigated the suicide rate (see: "The Jumping-Off Place," Chapter XXIV of *The American Jitters*). We interviewed a physician, the county coroner, and others, and then spent an afternoon looking through the suicide records, making notes from those strangely cryptic documents. The chapter that Wilson wrote on San Diego is notable for its description of the Coronado Hotel: "White and ornate as a wedding cake, clean, polished and trim as a ship, it makes a monument not unworthy to dominate the last blue concave dent in the shoreline before the United States gives way to Mexico."

Later, at Santa Barbara, Wilson asked me to read over the chapters on California, not as an amateur student of Californiana, but to determine what portions were libelous! Someday I hope to find time to write an article about my experiences as a cicerone, exhibiting, with pardonable pride, the wonders of Los Angeles to visiting New York journalists and writers. *(1937)*

Miss Greta Garbo, reaching San Diego after nine months in Sweden, electrified the world by nine words. They were spoken in bland reply to a question by a member of the press: "One never knows what time will bring, does one?" *(1933)*

Princess Zorene of the sun-tan colony in San Diego invited Sister Aimee Semple McPherson to tea. Princess Zorene is the inventor of "invisible panties," a mysterious arrangement that permits the princess to remain practically nude and still pass police inspection.

Sister Aimee, however, spurned the invitation, and Zorene was highly indignant: "I didn't ask her to take off her clothes; she was simply invited to tea." But Mrs. McPherson quoted from scripture: "I was naked and I hid myself" . . . "before the Fall man was naked and unashamed. But after he fell, he was ashamed. Even in Heaven people are clothed in white robes." And with this rejoinder she was "whisked off to deliver her afternoon sermon." *(1935)*

XI
Reading San Diego
Lawrence Clark Powell

————◆————

Lawrence Clark Powell, former head librarian at UCLA, teacher, author and critic, conducted *Westways*' column, "Western Books and Writers," from the early 1940s to the mid 1960s. In 1967 Powell began a series of travels through the West, collecting material for a *Westways* series on California authors, called "California Classics Reread." The characteristic Powell style—crisp, clear, witty, ironic —is evident in these selected reviews of San Diego books.

The California Historical Society issues a series of revised and enlarged reprints from its *Quarterly,* known as Special Publications. Number 22 in this series is Arthur Woodward's *Lances at San Pascual* ($4.00). This is probably the definitive account of the "battle" between General Kearny's dragoons and the native Californians, which occurred in San Diego County on November 23, 1846. Unlike the *opera bouffe* northern counterpart at Santa Clara the skirmish at San Pascual was bloody, with 10 Americans and one Californian losing their lives.

Woodward has carefully put together all the known facts and conjectures, down to the gruesome postscript of a warehouse mixup in which one of the survivors' coffined bones were sold to a stove-dealer, while a box of stove parts was shipped east and given a hero's burial.

(June, 1948)

Anyone who has ever fished off a Southern California ocean pier will relish James Clifford Safley's *Fisherman's Pier* (Stanford, $2.50), a collection of essays on his fellow anglers in or near San Diego. Mr. Safley is the managing editor of the *San Diego Union,* and he has a trained eye for copy. His vignettes are shrewd and sympathetic studies of the people who patiently seek to establish hook and line contact with watery creatures.

(June, 1948)

I am grateful to Judy Van der Veer—more about her and her books next month—for calling my attention to her neighbor George de Clyver Curtis's *Bees' Ways* (Houghton, $2.75). For a generation the venerable Harvard-schooled, former librarian Curtis has been a beekeeper on his homesteaded acres in the San Diego back country. In this modest and mellow book he has dressed much knowledge and wisdom in a style which is sheer pleasure to read. It is an informative and delightful book, nurtured in the sage-redolent foothills of Cuyamaca. If you keep bees you will find it useful; if, like myself, you merely keep honey, you will find it as sweet to savor. Black-and-white illustrations by Edwin Earle and a honey-colored binding are the final irresistible touches.

(June, 1949)

Although Max Miller and others have jointly covered the waterfront of San Diego County, to Judy Van der Veer alone belongs the back country. This was made clear in the four books which she published between 1936 and 1943—*The River Pasture, Brown Hills, November Grass* and *A Few Happy Ones*—and in the chapter which she contributed to *Pacific Coast Ranges*. Sooner or later these volumes are going to be called back into print. They are short works and could be gathered nicely between the covers of a single omnibus volume. In no other writing do we find such sensitive, faithful, and beautifully written vignettes of Southern

California hills, skies and seasons, animals and birds, and of the people who work the earth.

(July, 1949)

The relentless pressure of time and the prolificness of the modern printing press prevent a reviewer from reading every last word of every book that crosses his desk. I must confess to having been frightened by the length (751 pages) and the weight (5 lbs.) of a recent volume entitled *Memoirs* by Ed. Fletcher, so that I lifted it gingerly and sampled a few pages here and there. Whereupon I was lost. Back I turned to page one and read my eager way through to the end.

Here is a great pioneer story, told without literary style, but with sincerity and unflagging energy; the autobiography of Ed. Fletcher, who came to San Diego in the 1880s, is there yet, and still going strong. His pioneer work in developing water supplies, roads, agriculture, real estate and harbor, and his twelve years in the state senate, are recounted by Colonel Fletcher with magnificent gusto. Particularly choice is the story of how he "stole" for San Diego the monument of Cabrillo which his political foe, Governor Culbert Olson, had slated for erection in Oakland!

Fletcher's massive volume is lavishly illustrated with photographs and facsimiles of letters and documents illustrative of a career, in the course of which he knew everyone from the Prince of Wales to General MacArthur. The book is privately printed in a limited edition, "to be presented to our family, close friends and associates." . . . It is truly an important and primary source book on the economic development of the farthest Southwest corner of the U.S.A.

(August, 1952)

If it were not for the passionate vigilance of a few collectors in each generation, many books published privately in small editions would be swallowed by Time and lost forever. Down San Diego way such a collector is Wilmer B. Shields, who for many years has been specializing in books printed in or written about San Diego County, while at the same time his friend, Dr. John Adams of San Diego State College, has been compiling a bibliography of these San Diego imprints, the publication of which might well be underwritten as a cultural service by civic groups in the border city.

Last month we were in San Diego to inspect the new Public Library, with its two beautiful bas-relief sculptures by Donal Hord, and ended up in Wilmer Shields' study to see his most recent San Diego finds. There we found him gloating over what he regards as his all-time prize in this field, a copy of which he had winnowed out of the bibliographical chaff in the backroom of a charitable agency.

Printed in San Diego in 1909 and entitled *Good's Budget, the Adventures of an American Boy,* the volume is a Horatio Alger-like account of one Ned Winter, who sallies forth into the world to make his fortune and pay off the family mortgage. The frontispiece is a photograph of the author, himself a boy, bearing the signature "Goodwin J. Knight."

Instead of following a career of authorship, the writer of this lively work won a scholarship to Stanford, became an attorney and judge, and is now the governor of California—a career not without some of the Horatio Algeresque elements present in his rare juvenile work.

(October, 1954)

Another local periodical which has features of interest to non-agricultural Westways readers is *The Southern*

California Rancher, a monthly magazine founded twenty years ago by its editor, Philip S. Rush. Its special area is San Diego County and southern Riverside and Orange counties, and though its primary aim is at "citrus, avocado, field crop and row crop farmers, cattle and dairy ranchers, poultrymen, turkey men, rabbit and goat raisers," it contains articles on local history, and a book column. The cover of a recent issue reproduces a picture of the Huntington Library's precious Gutenberg Bible.

The cost of *The Southern California Rancher* is only one dollar a year, and there is a premium of a calendar, each month of which reproduces one of Editor Rush's beautiful photographs of the San Diego back country. . . .

(April, 1956)

People's pets are an index to their character. Cat people—I mean those who have cats—are like no others, and are often joined in argument with dog people. Cats are unaffectionate and independent, the latter say, and are countered with, dogs are messy and undiscriminating. The ideal situation is when cat people and dog people are one people, and Pussy and Rover and People are one big (mostly happy) family.

When this occurs and the people are bee people, too, that I say is the news of the month, just as an account of it all is our book of the month.

On this page in 1948 I hailed *Bees' Ways,* a learned and charming narrative about beekeeping in the San Diego back country by George De Clyver Curtis, a distinguished New Englander who homesteaded near Ramona in the year 1906 and is still there now, in his eighty-fourth year.

His *Cats' Tales and Dogs' Days* will vastly delight both cat people and dog people, nor will bee people be stung if they buy it, for there is a lively incident of what happened when two young turkey cocks got to fighting in the midst of the hives. Mostly, however, the book is about the Curtis's long line of Persian cats—at the time of writing they had kept only three, ages nineteen, sixteen and fifteen—and lovable packs of watchdogs, purebred and mongrel (New York: American Press, $3.00).

There is much affection in Curtis's writing and no sentimentality; here are the eternal joys and sorrows of keeping and losing pet animals, told in a down-to-earth, yet tender way by a highly educated man who has drawn both strength and solace from a ranch life close to the soil.

Incidentally, George Curtis's neighbor is Judy Van der Veer, whose earlier books, *The River Pasture, Brown Hills, November Grass,* and *A Few Happy Ones,* also portray this San Diego back country to the loving life.

(July, 1956)

The Huntington Library is the publisher of Andrew Rolle's *An American in California, the Biography of William Heath Davis, 1822-1909,* and the research for it was carried out by this energetic young professor of history at Occidental College, in libraries from Honolulu to Harvard ($4.25).

Davis was a trader and merchant, with Kanaka blood in his veins, who flourished in the Islands and on the California coast. His *Seventy-Five Years in California,* written in his old age, has long been a standard work of Californiana. He was the founder of American San Diego.

Andrew Rolle has written a model biography of the man, as well as a period study of mercantile life in nineteenth-century California, and to do this he dug through masses of source material. Writing the book was like assembling a jigsaw puzzle, using the myriad pieces of business records, correspondence, and contemporary accounts. The result is convincing, readable, and characteristic of the work to be expected from an historian trained under the twin mastership of Robert Glass Cleland and John Walton Caughey.

(December, 1956)

Scott O'Dell's *Country of the Sun: Southern California, an Informal History and Guide* (Crowell, $3.95) is the best book on the region since Carey McWilliams's *Southern California Country.* Although O'Dell lacks the sociological insight or intellectual power of McWilliams, he has a simpler and warmer feeling for people than the other has and a better flair for anecdotal narrative, derived from his skill as a novelist.

Country of the Sun is what its subtitle proclaims it to be: an informal history and guide. The counties included are Imperial, San Diego, Riverside, Orange, San Bernardino, Los Angeles, Ventura, Santa Barbara and Inyo. The history of each is given in terms of the people, not the forces, which made it; and, in doing this, the author works over old material in a fresh and exciting way. The account of Kate Sessions, the San Diegan who planted Balboa Park with the trees which make it today of such extraordinary beauty, is an example of O'Dell's personal approach to history. . . .

The trouble is, 300 pages are just not enough in which to do justice to this land.

Yet, as far as it goes, *Country of the Sun* is one of the few good books written about Southern California, and for the reason that Scott O'Dell savvies this neck of the woods. Not mean-eyed like a New Yorker, horrified like a New Englander, bug-eyed like a Nebraskan, or suffering from English jaundice, this *paisano* from Julian, San Diego County, loves his homeland, and the book he writes about it, while not a panegyric, is motivated by affection and not by scorn.

Country gentleman he is, too, for not once does Scott O'Dell mention that dirty four-letter word, s - - g.

(November, 1957)

Members of the San Diego Historical Society by now will have received volume 5, number 1 of the Society's quarterly publication. Compiled by James Mills, curator of the Junípero Serra Museum, it is called *Historical Landmarks of San Diego County*. I recommend it as glove-compartment equipment for motorists in the county, especially for those who prefer the free ways of the back roads to the regimentation of the freeways. Copies may be had for 50 cents from the Society at 2727 Presidio Drive, San Diego 3.

Three dollars is the amount of annual dues for membership in the San Diego Historical Society, bringing the quarterly publication, as well as local membership privileges especially to San Diego and neighboring residents. Application should be made to Wilmer Shields, Secretary, at the above address.

(May, 1959)

Some people born in the city can be happily only in the country, Judy Van der Veer observes, as well as the other way around. The trick is to know where you can be your happy self, and then try to make it economically possible. Miss Van der Veer was born and brought through high school in a city before she found her true life and love to be the country, where she has lived for more years than a gentleman should say.

How many times has this page referred to Judy Van der Veer's books about her loving life on the land, called for them to be reprinted, hoped she would write another? In the *River Pasture, Brown Hills, November Grass,* and *A Few Happy Ones* a reader will find the eternal verities told with simple artlessness, touched with compassion, and illuminated by a love of natural beauty.

These books have not yet been reprinted—they would fit nicely into a single omnibus volume—but this ranch woman who writes has at last added one to them. *My Valley in the Sky* is Judy Van der Veer's new book, and I suggest you order a copy to read, copy to lend, and a copy to put away against the day when it may go out of print (Messner, $3.50).

For those of you who are reading for the first time about Judy Van der Veer and wonder where her paradise is, I will say only that it is somewhere in the mountains northeast of San Diego. She wisely gives no explicit directions, for there is nothing more difficult for an author to deal with than literary tourists.

What is *My Valley in the Sky* about? Everyday life on the ranch, the author's niece Wowser, Pig, Goat, Don Roscoe the Stallion, assorted mares, goats, poodles, pinschers, and countless cats, and the things that happen to these creatures, ludicrous, painful, companionable, and the author's brooding compassion for them all.

The book has two villains: hunters and drought. Miss Van der Veer understands killing to eat, but not killing as "sport." In deer season nothing is safe: horses, cattle, and people. Damn fools from the city will shoot at anything that moves. Throughout the book stalks the drought that has plagued the back country periodically in recent years, relieved intermittently by the winter song of rain. When rain falls, Judy Van der Veer's prose sings with the running water. And now that her long literary drought is broken with this singing book, her fans are rejoicing, and new readers will be won.

By chance the same month brings a beautiful pamphlet about a holy place in the San Diego back country. *The Story of Misión San Antonio de Pala* is by Father J. M. Carillo, pastor of the mission, and it has been published by Dr. Horace Parker from his Paisano Press on Balboa Island (order from the Mission, Pala, California, $1.50, tax and postage included). . . .

(July, 1959)

An odd and out-of-the-way volume of pictures and words, also of interest to juveniles and grownups, is *A Dog Called Bum,* a resurrection by Marie Hitchcock and others of a legendary San Diego dog of the 1890s. It recalls a little volume about San Francisco dogs of bygone years—*The Story of Bummer and Lazarus* by Robert Ernest Cowan, published in 1938 by the Ward Ritchie Press and well deserving of a reprint.

(March, 1961)

"A life must be lived, and then it must be written, and then it must be read," quotes Martha Boaz from Phillips Brooks, at the beginning of her biography of Althea Warren, "before the power of the biography is complete."

As an enthusiast for books and people, as a woman of conviction and courage, and as city librarian of San Diego and then Los Angeles, Althea Warren lived the kind of life that gave Miss Boaz, dean of the University of Southern California School of Library Science, the title of her skillfully written book, *Fervent and Full of Gifts* (Scarecrow Press, $4.50).

Because of this biography, Miss Warren will live a second life in the minds and hearts of its readers. And they will be more than library school students, to whom nevertheless the book will be a kind of bible, for Althea Warren was far more than an able municipal administrator; she was a radiant personality surrounded by her own special aura of belief in the power of books to enrich, sustain, and delight. Few people failed to be moved by her. She was the kind of yea-saying librarian we need more of, equally at ease in a circle of children or encircled by city councilmen.

I have particular reason to remember and revere Althea Warren; it was she who led me into library work and gave me my first job.

(October, 1961)

The man who gets around San Diego County more than anyone I know is Philip S. Rush, publisher of the *Southern California Rancher* magazine. And he takes a camera with him everywhere he goes, favoring views of pastoral places rather than people. *Beautiful San Diego County* is a book of his photographs (Rush, 1134 30th Street, San Diego, $2.00). They will become increasingly nostalgic as the landscapes become peopled.

(January, 1962)

. . . *We come to several new books* about San Diego. *Time of the Bells* by Richard Pourade is the second volume in a sumptuous series on the history of San Diego, the first of which was called *The Explorers* (Union-Tribune, $9.50). This new work, also carefully researched, well written, and lavishly illustrated from photographs, drawings, paintings, maps, and documents, treats of the Franciscan efforts to Christianize the Indians from Yuma west, culminating in the mission establishments of San Diego and San Luis Rey. James S. Copley deserves credit for commissioning and subsidizing this fine series, the volumes of which cost far more to produce than the price for which they sell.

Jerry McMullen combines San Diego newspaper work and museum directing with maritime history. His *Paddle Wheel Days in California* and *Ships of the Redwood Coast* are standard works. In a new book called *Star of India, the Log of an Iron Ship,* he has written the life history of a windjammer with an iron hull, launched at Ramsey, Isle of Man, in 1863 (Howell-North, $3.75). She is now being restored as a museum vessel in San Diego harbor, the dedication to be held next year upon the centennial of her birth.

Our Book of Jubilee, 1886–1961, edited by Ben F. Dixon, is about San Diego's Central Christian Church, and is subtitled "The Life Story of a Downtown Church, with Its Historic Setting in a Spanish Background, the Protestant Advent, and the Coming of the Disciples." (Plastic $5.00, cloth $4.00). It contains much early history and biography and reproduces many early photographs of San Diego places and people. . . .

(February, 1962)

Up to now the late Colonel Ed. Fletcher's *Memoirs* has been my favorite southern California booster book. It has been joined by Oscar Cotton's *The Good Old Days* (Exposition Press, $4.75). Both are San Diego books. Cotton came there in 1907 and is still going strong. Real estate was also his specialty. Between

Fletcher and Cotton, I would guess they subdivided (at a profit) most of the county from Yuma to Coronado. *The Good Old Days* takes the author from his origins as a stereopticon lecturer, dealer in concrete blocks, and promoter of the expositions of 1915 and 1935, to his golden wedding anniversary reception on Point Loma. The many photographic illustrations are of prime local interest.

(February, 1963)

Readers may recall that last month's page began with an account of what we called the most beautiful book ever printed in Arizona—the Perceval-Lockett *Navajo Sketch Book,* superbly composed in type, with numerous illustrations in color and black and white.

This month we salute a humbler southern California production, economically composed on the varityper and photographically reproduced by Elena Quinn in her shop at P.O. Box No. 14, Downey, California.

Written by her husband, Charles Russell Quinn, this modest yet handsome volume, *Mesa Grande Country,* subtitled "Some Observations about the Quiet Life and Times on a High Plateau in the San Diego Back Country," is about the kind of place Russ Leadabrand has specialized in seeking out. Even when publicized by him and the Quinns, such places will never be thronged by tourists, for the reason that they are not spectacular and do not offer the attractions which many people find necessary in order to keep occupied while in the country.

The Mesa Grande is high, wide and lonesome, with few people, including a small band of indigenous Indians, cattle, oaks, and an occasional eucalyptus of great age and majesty. In this fine book the Quinns have gathered a wealth of historical lore and documentation, including pictures from the Indian collection of Edward H. Davis, a photographer to rank with Adam Clark Vroman.

Mesa Grande Country is published in a limited hardbound edition at $10 and in wrappers at $4.00. It is a labor of love; and I hope that its reception will encourage Elena and Charles Quinn to compile similar books about other parts of southern California unsung by the All Year Club. . . .

(March, 1963)

Pioneering in Dulzura by Dorothy Clark Schmid is a well-written history of the back country due east of San Diego and bordered by Mexico, a great bee country when enough rain falls to bring out the blossoms (Robert Knapp, P.O. Box 7234, San Diego, hardbound $3.50). Mrs. Schmid, a native daughter of Dulzura, has based her work on both archival research and personal interviews. Illustrations are from early and contemporary photographs. It is a good example of the kind of work that every community in the state should sponsor and every reader of this page should buy and read.

Also from down San Diego way is *The Silver Dons* by Richard F. Pourade, the third volume in the noble series on California's early history centering on San Diego, commissioned by James S. Copley (Union-Tribune Publishing Co., $9.50). This latest work by the editor emeritus of the *San Diego Union* deals with the period between the secularization of the missions in 1835 and the Civil War, the so-called golden age of the ranchos, and is equally well written and lavishly illustrated.

(December, 1963)

The Quinns have done it again—produced a beautiful piece of Californiana to sell for only a dollar. Charles Russell Quinn's *The Story of Mission Santa Ysabel,* published by Elena Quinn, P.O. Box 14, Downey, California, is another of Mrs. Quinn's triumphs with the varityper.

Where is Santa Ysabel? Deep in the San Diego back country on State Highway 78. Though founded by the Franciscans, the mission is conducted today by the Sons of the Sacred Heart. The present church is modern, dating from 1924; the spirit and the atmosphere are timeless.

(May, 1964)

Another local writer-publisher is also on our monthly honors list. He is Dr. Horace M. Parker, the Balboa Island veterinarian, whose beat is the Brush Country of Riverside-San Diego counties. His Paisano Press has produced a series of worthwhile items of Southern Californiana and Southwestern Americana.

Now "Doc" Parker has started a new series of booklets called "Paisano Press Libritos." Number 1 is *The Historic Valley of Temecula; the Early Indians of Temecula.* It contains attractive lithographed illustrations from drawings of places and artifacts, and sells for a mere $1.00. The Paisano Press is at Box 85, Balboa Island, California.

Working our way south brings us to still another local devotee, the late Philip S. Rush, editor and publisher of the excellent monthly journal called *Southern California Rancher* at P.O. Box N, San Diego.

From the back columns of this periodical, Rush gathered into book form a series of articles entitled *Some Old Ranchos and Adobes* (published by the author, $5.00). The emphasis is on San Diego County and its neighbors, Riverside and Orange; the modern photographs of the old landmarks were taken by Rush. His publications are not as attractively produced as those of the Quinns and Parker, but they are no less dedicated to the recognition and preservation of our local heritage.

(August, 1965)

The rest of the month's books are a mixed shelf, all of unusual variety and interest. It is good to note the publication of the fifth volume in Richard F. Pourade's history of San Diego. *Gold in the Sun,* it is called, and it covers the first quarter century of our era (Union-Tribune, $9.50). Like its four predecessors, this latest volume is sumptuously produced, with many photographs and lavish colored reproductions of paintings. These were San Diego's years of developing water resources and harbor, and of the Exposition of 1915, full of nostalgia for one who, as a boy of nine, marveled at the buildings, the electric go-carts, and the hungry pigeons. The go-carts have long since gone; many of the noble buildings and the now venerable trees remain in Balboa Park; as for the pigeons, they are still there in the umpteenth generation.

(January, 1966)

For twenty years and more, Professor John R. Adams of San Diego State College, aided and encouraged by the county's leading book collector, Wilmer Shields, has been working on a bibliography of San Diego County books. Now at long last his devoted labor has born fruit. Adams's *Books and Authors of San Diego, a Checklist,* has been published by the State College Press ($7.50). Its 250 pages list 1,939 books and pamphlets, arranged by author and by subject, with references to reviews and biographical material, constituting a veritable encyclopedia of San Diegana.

Thanks to the zeal of Wilmer Shields, most of the items listed by Professor Adams have been preserved from the destruction which overtakes much local printed material because no one bothers to preserve it. The Shields Collection is destined for the California Room of the San Diego Public Library, an institution which has never failed to recognize its obligation as a cultural depository.

(July, 1966)

Strictly homemade and local is Gordon Stuart's *San Diego Back Country, 1901,* another of the books written, set in type, and printed by the hands of this octogenarian philosopher. His rambling, folksy reminiscences are of the Escondido-Poway area at the turn of the century and later. This spiral-bound book of 241 pages took Stuart three years to print, and is well worth the $5.00 it sells for from the author, at 1015 Galloway Street, Pacific Palisades. When writing, ask for his list of earlier books, likewise handmade, for there aren't many such these days.

(June, 1967)

Scripps is another great philanthropic name perpetuated by a branch of the University of California. Early in the century, E. W. Scripps, the newspaper monarch, and his sister, Ellen Browning Scripps, added their resources to the struggling marine biological station at La Jolla, and it grew into the world-renowned Scripps Institution of Oceanography, later becoming the nucleus of the proliferating University of California at San Diego.

A superb history of the development has been written by Helen Raitt and Beatrice Moulton and titled *Scripps Institution of Oceanography, the First Fifty Years* (Ward Ritchie Press, $9.50). This is no dry, academic treatise, but rather a history in terms of those pioneer scientists, led by W. E. Ritter, whose learning and love brought greatness to their work.

Current generalizations about the statewide university tend to overlook the creative role the university has played in the rise of California. This book should be read by those who may have lost sight of the University's real and continuing value.

(December, 1967)

About *Westways*

The predecessor of *Westways*, *Touring Topics,* was started in Los Angeles in 1909 as a "house organ" to keep the thousand or so members of the Automobile Club of Southern California informed on road conditions, new cars and gadgets, automobile legislation, and club-sponsored tours and outings. The early magazine consisted in the main of accounts of "gay motor parties" or "happy auto caravans" up to the mountains or out along the coast.

After World War I, the broadening scope of the magazine included articles describing in greater detail the wonders of rural California and the West—areas which rapidly were being opened to motor travel. By the mid 1920s, more and more space was devoted to accounts of local history. First person adventure tales were welcomed. Old-timers were sought out for their tales, even short stories were occasionally admitted. Humorous social commentaries and reviews of entertainment and the arts were also part of its pages.

On its 25th birthday in 1934, the magazine's name was changed to *Westways,* to reflect more accurately its cosmopolitan subject matter. In subsequent years, *Westways* has continued to present articles on a wide range of subjects, balancing history, travel, entertainment, and current events with items of particular interest to the automobile owner.

*Tales of adventure, courage, and of man's eternal
curiosity which pushed him on to the frontier*

FROM BALLANTINE'S
COMSTOCK SERIES

COMMITTEE OF VIGILANCE: Revolution in San Francisco, 1851, George R. Stewart $1.25

In meticulous detail, the succession of events which preceded the formation of the Committee of Vigilance and
the administration of justice under its unprecedented
100-day rule.

EAST OF THE GIANTS, George R. Stewart $1.25

The turbulent birth of the state of California—its
struggles with powerful church interests, night raids by
Indians, invasions by the White man, and the decisive
war and separation from Mexico—culminating in the
discovery of gold. "The best novel yet on early
California."

—Joseph Henry Jackson

DRIFTWOOD VALLEY,
   Theodora C. Stanwell-Fletcher $1.25

An amazing true-life adventure of a young naturalist and
her trapper husband, twentieth century pioneers in the
remote wilderness of the North, told with wonder, vio-
lence, and enchantment. "An utterly fascinating record."

—J. H. Jackson
San Francisco Chronicle

THE LAND OF LITTLE RAIN, Mary Austin $1.25

A colorful portrait of the unchanging border regions of
Southern California and Arizona and an early plea for
the preservation of that beauty. "This book sings of a
beautiful land. The song is a love song."

—Malcolm McKenna